The First Ashanti War
1823-31

The First Ashanti War 1823-31
The Conflict Between the British Army and the
Natives of West Africa

Narrative of the Ashantee War;
With a View of the Present State of the Colony
of Sierra Leone

H. I. Ricketts

The First Ashanti Campaign

J. W. Fortescue

The First Ashanti War 1823-31
The Conflict Between the British Army and the Natives of West Africa
Narrative of the Ashantee War;
With a View of the Present State of the Colony of Sierra Leone
by H. I. Ricketts
The First Ashanti Campaign
by J. W. Fortescue

FIRST EDITION

First published under the titles
Narrative of the Ashantee War;
With a View of the Present State of the Colony of Sierra Leone
and
A History of the British Army Vol 11 (Extract)

Leonaur is an imprint of Oakpast Ltd

Copyright in this form © 2014 Oakpast Ltd

ISBN: 978-1-78282-357-5 (hardcover)
ISBN: 978-1-78282-358-2 (softcover)

http://www.leonaur.com

Publisher's Notes

The views expressed in this book are not necessarily those of the publisher.

Contents

Preface	7
Appointment of Sir Charles MacCarthy	11
The Expedition Against the Ashantees Defeated	20
Active Preparations for War	28
Captain Ricketts Takes Charge of the Army	44
Advance of the Ashantees	49
Engagement with the Ashantees	57
The General Departs for Sierra Leone	67
Terms of Peace Proposed	78
Conclusion of a Final Peace	92
BRIEF VIEW OF THE PRESENT STATE OF THE COLONY OF SIERRA LEONE	
Succession of Governors	102
Commercial Pursuits	111
THE FIRST ASHANTI CAMPAIGN	
The Rise of the Ashanti	123

Preface

The following narrative was originally written on the spot, without any view to publication, but having been subsequently submitted to the inspection of competent persons, it is now printed in conformity with their opinion; and it is to be hoped that the events related, as well as that part of the coast described, will be deemed sufficiently interesting at this particular period, when, owing to various causes, the public attention has been directed to Africa and her population.

The author suffered shipwreck on that coast, and lost many documents which could not be recovered; but he has endeavoured, by unremitting exertions, in some measure, to supply the deficiency.

The authors long residence in that country, and the various official situations which he there filled, enable him to present a correct account of the origin and final termination of those disastrous contentions, which for so long a period desolated the African shores, and which he sincerely hopes are now for ever closed.

In submitting, therefore, this narration of facts, he trusts that it will be favourably received; and had not Providence left him the only surviving officer who witnessed most of the events on the Gold Coast, he would not have produced these pages, which are now published only from a sense of public duty.

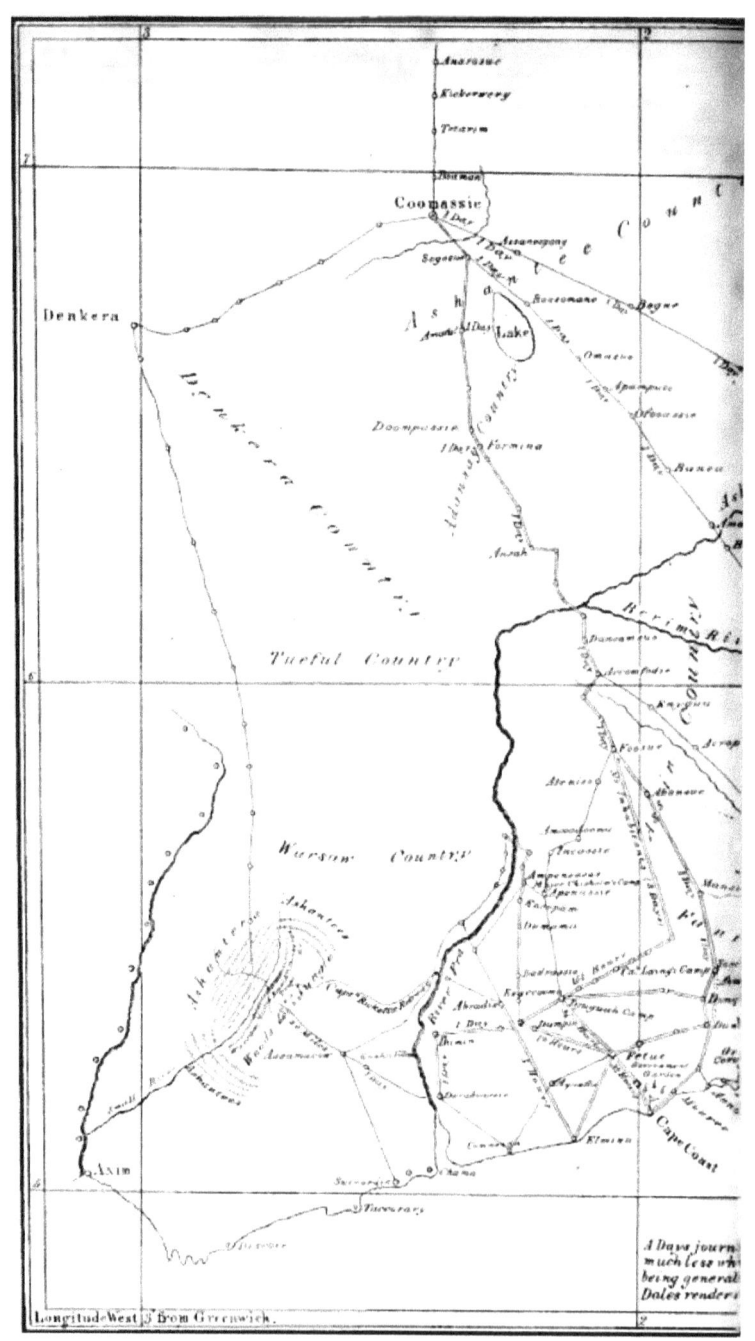

THE GOLD COAST AND THE

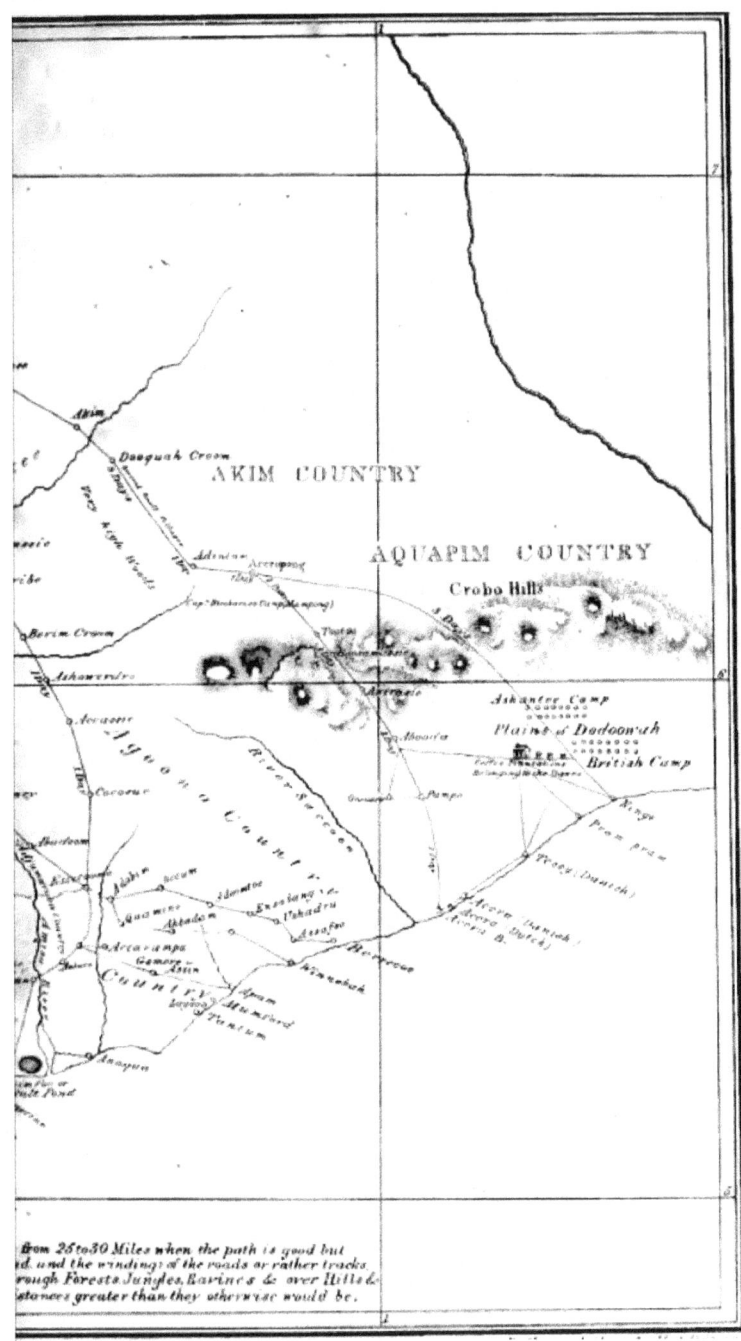

INTERIOR OF THE COUNTRY

CHAPTER 1

Appointment of Sir Charles MacCarthy

The late Sir Charles MacCarthy having been appointed Governor in Chief of the British settlements on the western coast of Africa, situated between twenty degrees north, and twenty degrees south latitude, returned to the colony of Sierra Leone, from England, whither he had been for a few months on leave, after having passed many years of his life in unwearied exertions for the benefit and improvement of the unfortunate natives of that country. He embarked on board His Majesty's ship the *Iphigenia*. Commodore Sir Robert Mends, on the 11th of March, 1822, and sailed for the Gold Coast to take possession of the forts which had been recently transferred from the African Company to government.

On the morning of the 27th of March he landed from the *Iphigenia* at Dixcove, where he was received by a numerous body of the inhabitants, who, as soon as the proclamation was read and explained to them, expressed their joy and satisfaction by loud and repeated acclamations. His Excellency then returned to the frigate, and reached Cape Coast Roads on the next morning, and on landing was received by thousands of the natives who were anxious to witness the change of government so long expected. On the 29th, the new charter and proclamation were read, the ships of war decorated with flags, and the guns of the castle fired a royal salute, accompanied with great rejoicing among all classes of the people. On the morning of the 30th, His Excellency re-embarked and dropped down to Annamaboe and landed, but returned in the evening to proceed to Accra, where he arrived on the 2nd of April and remained till the 11th, when he embarked and returned to Cape Coast Castle.

Sir Charles was highly delighted with the beautiful appearance of the country, but his stay on the Gold Coast was short, his presence being required at Sierra Leone. Since his arrival nothing had been heard from Coomassie: the Ashantees still carried on their trade to Elmina, Annamaboe, and Accra; but to Cape Coast they had not traded for a considerable period, owing to the following circumstances: the King of Ashantee, at the head of a powerful army, having subdued Bentooko, a country towards the interior of Ashantee, and killed the king, sent to Cape Coast to announce the event, and to ask for presents of powder, rum, and cloth, to assist him in making a splendid entry into his capital of Coomassie.

This was supposed to be an artifice on his part, to endeavour to discover how the Cape Coast people were affected towards him, and whether they were attached to his cause, the Fantees having, on apportioning to the different towns the sums which were required to make up a demand upon them by the King of Ashantee, included Cape Coast, but the people there refused to contribute anything whatever towards the settlement of the claim, and made it appear, at a public meeting held in the hall of the castle, that their connection with the Fantees never authorized such a demand, which they stated, if submitted to on this occasion, would subject them to a similar imposition, should any future claim be made on the Fantees. This decision, with many additions, was reported to the King of Ashantee.

The Cape Coast people being aware that the King of Ashantee could not without sufficient grounds make a direct demand upon them, yet seeing that it would be an unwise policy to refuse his request, sent him a present of fifty ounces of gold. Not long after this a similar message from the king was sent to the people of Commenda, where was an abandoned English fort; the messengers called at Cape Coast on their way to that place, and made known their mission in the public hall: they stated that they were sent by the king, to the Commendas, to communicate to them his great success in the late campaign, and as the king was about entering his capital, he required from them for that occasion cloth, powder, and rum, to the amount of one hundred ounces of gold (400*l*.)

The extreme poverty of these people was represented to the messengers, and they were told that there was no likelihood of their obtaining anything from the Commendas, that would be acceptable to the king, for that they had not as yet been able to discharge the debt of seventy ounces of gold due to the Cape Coast people, who had advanced that sum, to enable them to settle a former demand of the king. The messengers however proceeded to Commenda, where they were met by the inhabitants of that place outside of the town, but the nature of their message was so irritating, that the people refused to allow them to enter it, declaring they would rather perish than submit to such oppression.

The Ashantee messengers returned to Cape Coast, and one of them was dispatched to relate the result of their visit to the king; the principal observing that insulted as he had been, he could not think of returning to Coomassie. The king returned for answer, that if the Cape Coast people did not give him immediate satisfaction for the insult offered to him by the Commendas, whom he denominated their dependants, he could not but look to them for redress, and would send down an army to destroy their town. The governor replied that the Cape Coast people had not been guilty of any offence against the King of Ashantee, that they were by no means accessory to the conduct of the Commendas, nor ought they to suffer for their act of delinquency; and he added, that if the king commenced hostilities against the Cape Coast people, he should consider him as an enemy, and would afford them all the protection in his power.

On the 5th of January, 1820, a nephew of the King of Ashantee arrived with a numerous retinue for the purpose of negotiating the difference with the people of Commenda and Cape Coast. After recapitulating the particulars already mentioned, he proceeded to demand on the part of the king from the Cape Coast people sixteen hundred ounces of gold, on the plea that they abetted the Commendas in their insolent conduct to his messengers, also the sum of sixteen hundred ounces, in consequence of the governor having broken the treaty, as they said, by not procuring the king satisfaction from the Commendas and Cape Coast people. The Ashantees were asked in reply, whether they had ever heard of any sum having been paid for the purchase of a peace by the governor of the Coast to any King of Ashantee, or to any other native of Africa.

This question being answered in the negative, they were then informed that this was not the time to make any such concession; and if they persisted in their insulting demands, the sooner they returned to Coomassie the better; that however anxious the government might be to continue friends with the King of Ashantee, such terms could not for a moment be admitted, adding that the King of England had sent Mr. Dupuis out for the purpose of visiting the King of Ashantee, and that he had been detained at Cape Coast a considerable time on account of the existing differences, but that he was ready to proceed on the faith of the treaty made with Mr. Bowditch, conceiving it still to be in full force. The Ashantee chief and his attendants, together with the Cape Coast chiefs, assembled a second time in the hall, but nothing decisive took place; the Ashantees however, urged their claim on the castle with less confidence. It is stated by Mr. Dupuis in his work, that the king gave up his claim, when his majesty saw him at Coomassie.[1]

The Cape Coast people having been enabled in June, by the assistance which was offered to them by the castle, to make their final payment to the King of Ashantee, it was expected that his chief would have taken his departure for Coomassie. He however, still continued at Cape Coast, stating as his motive that he had received further orders from the king to examine into the grounds of a difference between the Cape Coast people and the Fantees, which was this, one of the principal *caboceers* of Fantee named Paintry, had been placed at Donquah, (a Fantee town,) by the King of Ashantee as a reward for the part he had taken in the king's war with that tribe, and actuated by the refusal of the Cape Coast natives to contribute fifty ounces of gold as their share of the sum demanded from the Fantees, at the conclusion of the war, a matter in which the Cape Coast people had no concern, Paintry sent an armed force, and destroyed a village belonging to a native of Cape Coast named Tando, and carried off the greater number of the people who resided there.

The person who headed the body came to Cape Coast about nine months afterwards, when Tando managed to secure him, together with several of his attendants, and to satiate his revenge, destroyed himself with gunpowder with the man and many others who were in the house at the same time. This the Ashantee chief was directed by the king to decide; and to demand a fine of one hundred *penguins* of gold (1000*l*.) from the party he adjudged to be wrong: the Ashantee chief,

---

1. "I want the people to serve me, and serve white men. It is true I told the governor he must pay me gold, but now I see your face I am willing to relinquish that. Cape Coast, however, must give me gold, for they are my people, and if they will be insolent I must punish them; for unless I do so, all these countries will laugh, and say what kind of king is this? The governor knows I am right, for he now sends word the people are unable to pay sixteen hundred ounces, and that if I will abate something it will be paid. 'What I tell you,' added the king, noticing my surprise, 'is very true; here is the messenger,' pointing to the man who brought the message up."—*Dupuis' Journal of a Residence in Ashantee.*

in order to carry the orders he had received into effect, required the appearance of Paintry (the Fantee *caboceer* already alluded to) at Cape Coast, which he declined complying with, but came to Moorie, about four miles to leeward of Cape Coast.

These events occurred in the beginning of April, 1821, and on the 9th of the same month intelligence was received at Cape Coast, that a black man belonging to that place had been cruelly murdered at Moorie. The troops of the castle were in consequence immediately assembled and marched to Moorie, where they found about two thousand men assembled, and saw the mangled remains of the victim. As soon as the troops entered the town, a fire was opened upon them; but the Fantees, who had assembled to assist the Ashantees in their demand on the Cape Coast people, retired as the troops advanced and returned the fire. As soon as the Ashantees, who had taken up their quarters in the vicinity of Cape Coast, heard that the governor had sent an armed force against the people assembled at Moorie, they hastened after them, and finding the Fantees had given way, rallied them and took up a position, with an apparent determination to oppose the troops returning to Cape Coast. The governor being informed of this, assembled all the force he could collect, which was between three and four thousand men, of the adjoining town and adjacent dependant villages, headed by some of the company's officers and carrying the British flag; but the Fantees and Ashantees retired upon their approach.

They had fifty killed, among whom was Paintry the chief, whose body was brought to Cape Coast and buried westward, outside of the castle, close to the walls of the ramparts where the flag-staff stands: some time afterwards it was disinterred and allowed to be taken to his own country. The loss on the part of our troops was only two killed, and a few slightly wounded. Trade with the Ashantees was now totally stopped, and it was not thought safe to venture beyond the bounds of Cape Coast, unless in large parties.

A short time after messengers arrived at Cape Coast from the King of Ashantee, who stated that his majesty had heard that Paintry had been killed, and that he was directed to enquire of the governor, why this had been done without his being acquainted with it, and that they had brought the book of treaties, that the governor might look at them: the messengers being asked for what purpose, replied because the king said the governor had broken the law. The whole of the circumstances were however explained to the messengers for the satisfaction of the king, and in conclusion he was plainly told, that the government of Cape Coast acknowledged no right on the part of the King of Ashantee to interpose in any matter which occurred within the jurisdiction of the fort.

On the 21st of August a party of Ashantees arrived at Cape Coast with a message to the governor, stating that a misrepresentation of the affair at Moorie had been made to the king, and that his majesty was so satisfied with the true account of the particulars given to his messengers, that he dropped the affair entirely, and had given orders that every obstruction to the direct communication of the Ashantees with Cape Coast should be immediately removed. When however Sir Charles MacCarthy assumed the government of the Gold Coast, the Ashantee trade had not revived at Cape Coast: the king, at the commencement of the differences, had strictly forbidden his subjects to traffic with any people of that place. Though they frequently walk that road in their way to Elmina, our merchants were not able to remove the injunction against them. Some Ashantees came to Cape Coast in January, previous to Sir Charles's arrival, with an insolent message to Mr. Smith the late governor, and required him to swear on whiteman's book (the bible) and also the people of Cape Coast, that they were the good friends of the king. They were sent back to Coomassie, on Sir Charles's arrival, but they did not return, nor did he ever receive any message from them.

The natives of Cape Coast had, during these disputes, built a mud wall loop-holed from the sea beach on the right of the town, across the hills to the sea beach on the left; inclosing within it the town; and the African Company's government had hastily erected a Martello tower of mud and clay, on a hill in the immediate vicinity, to fortify which Sir George Collier landed some guns from his majesty's ship *Tartar*.

Such was the state of affairs on the Gold Coast when Sir Charles MacCarthy, agreeably to instructions from his majesty, took upon himself the government of that part of the coast. He sailed for Sierra Leone about the 12th of May, leaving particular instructions to cultivate and cherish a good understanding with all the natives around, to fulfil the treaties by the due payment of customs, and to impress on their minds that Great Britain had no other object but to encourage their commerce and industry. Sir Charles, with the impression that he should at his next visit find the country in the full enjoyment of peace, was with the most bitter feelings of disappointment informed in November following, that the chief of the Ashantees, after receiving by his messengers the usual presents, had, in breach of the treaties entered into with Mr. Bowdich, and afterwards with Mr. Dupuis, and in defiance of the established usages of the country during peace, without any application whatever to Major Chisholm, the commandant of the Gold Coast, employed his agents to kidnap a *mulatto* man, (a sergeant in the Royal African colonial corps) who was on duty at Annamaboe; the unfortunate man was carried a prisoner to Donquah in the Fantee country, fifteen miles at the back of Annamaboe fort, and there detained in irons.

This atrocious violation of the existing treaties was said to have been occasioned by a dispute which had taken place between an Ashantee trader, and the sergeant inside of Annamaboe fort in the month of May preceding. This affair had been inquired into at the time by the officer commanding the fort, and a justice of the peace, when it was satisfactorily proved that the Ashantee began the altercation by cursing the sergeant's master, who had retorted in similar expressions and turned the Ashantee out of the fort. From the time of Sir Charles MacCarthy's return to the Gold Coast from Sierra Leone in the early part of December, 1822, until February 1823, it was daily reported and circulated by the Ashantee *caboceers* at Dunquah and the Fantees, that their king (Osai Tootoo Quamina,) disapproved of the proceedings of his agents, and had ordered messengers to send down the sergeant, and as no precedent of a similar outrage was known, that was generally credited.

On the 2nd of February, it was ascertained that a son of the late king had been sent down by Osai from Coomassie, with one of his executioners, to put the sergeant to death, and to send the jaw-bone, skull, and one of the arms of the victim to him. This murder was committed on the 1st of February. His Excellency now considered it to be his duty to punish the perpetrators of such an atrocious act, and not wishing to involve the innocent with the guilty (the Fantees, who from the weakness or treachery of their chiefs had ceased to have a will of their own,) postponed assembling a force to attack those Ashantees who had been prominent in the perpetration of the crime; in the mean time he proceeded to Annamaboe to arrange matters for chastising the murderers, and he went by a new road which had been formed by subscription during his absence through the country.

He and his suite were conveyed in carriages drawn by natives, six to each vehicle, which accommodated two persons: the carriages were drawn by these men at the rate of six miles an hour, which, considering the unfinished state of the road, was astonishing, and the more so, as they were not at all fatigued on their arrival at Annamaboe. Neither horses, donkeys, nor mules, thrive on the Gold Coast. These animals have frequently been brought there from other parts of the Coast, but always died in a short time after being landed. At Accra, where the ships of the squadron are chiefly supplied with live stock, consisting of a small breed of cows and bullocks, with sheep and turkeys, obtained near the River Volta, they answer much better than at any other of the European possessions of the Gold Coast; and horses have been known to live there for several years.

The manner in which the Europeans travel in the vicinity of the forts where the road will allow of it, and they possess the means, is that which has been just described, and where the paths are narrow, they are carried in what is called a hammock, which is a piece of board about two feet in length, and half as broad, having two holes at each end fastened to a bamboo pole, very tight but strong, leaving sufficient room between, to enable the traveller who sits sideways on the board, with his feet resting on a smaller board below, dependant from the other, leaning his chest against the pole, and resting his arms on it, which is carried alternately on the shoulders and heads of two men. The native chiefs travel in this manner, and also in baskets made like a child's cradle, in which they can recline at full length, or sit up, the basket is also carried on the heads of men.

His Excellency's reception by the natives was extremely flattering, and on his leaving Annamaboe on the 10th, the young and old of both sexes followed him a great distance from the town, evincing the warmest regard and attachment to him and the British government: a great number of the inhabitants accompanied His Excellency as far as Ackertaccuah River, halfway, where he halted, and the natives of the country prompted by curiosity hastened to the spot; nearly a hundred people from Cape Coast were also assembled there to offer him their services as an honorary escort to Cape Coast Castle; the inhabitants of the villages shewed their hospitality by bringing large quantities of palm wine; each party of the natives was headed by a chief who individually insisted on swearing mutual friendship and support on His Excellency's sword, after the custom of their countries.

His Excellency then moved on for Cape Coast Castle, where he arrived about four o'clock in the afternoon. On his entrance into the town, the people had collected in vast numbers; the streets and hills were crowded by all classes, and cheering, shouting, firing of muskets, beating of drums, and the sounding of horns, manifested the sincerity of their attachment to his person, and their devotion to the interest and welfare of the government.

CHAPTER 2

The Expedition Against the Ashantees Defeated

It was ascertained on the 21st that Adookoo the king, and the principal chiefs of the Fantees, with their attendants, had returned from Donquah to their homes, and that the Ashantee prince and a few of his captains who were present at the murder of the sergeant, with their followers, amounting to two or three hundred only, remained at Donquah. No time was lost in forming an expedition, and without any previous notice being given to the regulars, the natives of the town of Cape Coast, and the volunteers who were called into the castle to receive their ammunition at 6 o'clock, were all on the march before seven in the evening.

From the treachery, however, or imbecility of the guides, the troops which ought to have reached Donquah, twenty miles from Cape Coast, at four o'clock the next morning, lost the right road, and, after excessive fatigue, and want of every sort of provisions, were suddenly attacked under a heavy fire by a numerous force of Ashantees and Fantees, ambushed in a thick covered wood, on both sides of a very narrow rugged path; but the advanced guard, consisting of a few men of the 2nd West India regiment, under the command of Captain Laing, Royal African corps, and Ensign Wetherell, of the 2nd West India regiment, returned the fire and moved onward, but finding that they had been led into a different direction from Donquah, it was conceived advisable that the expedition should fall back on Annamaboe.

In this affair there were six men killed; one officer, Lieutenant Swanzy, Royal African corps, thirty-eight men wounded, and four missing. Scarcely had the Ashantees murdered the sergeant, when they mustered several Fantee *caboceers* to go to Annamaboe and Cape Coast, to desire the natives living there under the protection of the forts, to take fetish, to be true to their chief, alluding to the King of Ashantee, but which they rejected. After the engagement at Donquah, some men of importance from the Fantees went to Annamaboe on the same business.

It appears that His Majesty's government, anxious to keep open the intercourse which had been made with the Ashantees by Mr. Bowdich, appointed Mr. Dupuis consul to Coomassie, who proceeded to the Ashantee capital in February, 1820, and in his treaty with His Sable Majesty, sanctioned the claims of Osai Tootoo Quamina over the liberty of the whole Fantee nation, which country is as extensive and as populous as that of Ashantee; he also inserted in the supplementary articles of the treaty, that "it is hereby expressly stipulated, that the natives of Cape Coast Town being subjects to the King of Ashantee, are excluded from participating in the benefits of either of the treaties, as the king is resolved to eradicate from his dominions the seeds of disobedience and insubordination."[2]

The natives of Cape Coast were never conquered by the Ashantees: they have enjoyed freedom under the protection of the British flag for nearly two centuries, although in some instances they have been permitted or advised to make free gifts to the King of Ashantee, who demanded, in 1820, sixteen hundred ounces of gold dust from the castle, and as much from the inhabitants: to the first a refusal was given; on the second demand on the people, whose inability to pay such a fine being fully known to the governor and council of the African company, they lent them two hundred ounces, well knowing the inconvenience that would result to them from a dispute with the King of Ashantee, with whose power they were unable to contend; and although they would have found protection within the range of the castle guns, yet in the event of a war, they must have withdrawn from the interior, abandoned their village and plantations, and become dependant on exterior supplies for the necessaries of life.

On the 14th of April, His Excellency and suite embarked on board the *Owen Glendower*, Commodore Sir Robert Mends, and the squad-

---

2. Originally this monarch intended to have written a letter to the king of England, containing sentiments to this effect, but changing his intention after the general treaty had been signed, he desired his ambassadors to explain his sentiments at the British court as they are here recorded. The propriety of writing them down in a treaty, he affirmed was manifest, as the governor and white men would know his immutable policy, and the public sentiments of his captains.—*Dupuis' Narrative of a Residence in Ashantee.*

ron sailed for Accra; although His Excellency set off at an earlier hour than he intended, there was a large assemblage of persons to pay a tribute of respect to an officer who had endeared himself to every class of society; the acclamations were general, and expressed those sentiments that proceeded alone from sincere respect.

In consequence of the *Owen Glendower* having lost all her topmasts on the 14th by a tornado, the strongest gust of wind ever remembered by the oldest inhabitants on this coast, the squadron did not arrive at Accra until Wednesday, the 16th. On His Excellency's landing, the inhabitants of the town of Danish, Dutch, and British Accra, which are close to each other, evinced great joy. The men kept up an incessant fire of musquetry, the females sang and swept the path before him, others sprinkled it with water.

On the 26th, Dr. Nicoll, deputy inspector of hospitals, and in charge of the civil and military medical department on the western coast of Africa, departed this life on board his majesty's ship *Cyrene*; he had been dangerously ill a long time, and as it was thought that a change of air, and a voyage at sea would afford him some benefit, he embarked on the 14th at Cape Coast, on board the *Cyrene*, Captain Percy Grace, who, with his officers, paid him every mark of esteem and regard, to which he was so deservedly entitled.

In him the governor in chief, and all those who had the welfare of Africa at heart, lost a friend. By his unwearied exertions to promote the cause of humanity, by his unbounded liberality, and by the goodness of his heart, he contributed much to raise in the minds of the natives of Africa, a high respect for a British officer.

It appeared that the King of Ashantee had sent messengers to the governor of Elmina, thanking him for all favours, and saying that Governor MacCarthy was wrong in his palaver, and he advised that Cape Coast Castle should be enlarged, as he intended to drive the English into the sea; he also recommended that they should arm the fishes of the sea, for all would be of no avail against the army which he intended to bring against them. About the 28th, His Excellency left Accra for Cape Coast, where he arrived on the 8th of May. He was shortly after informed that a party of Ashantees had arrived at Danish Accra to purchase gunpowder which had been prohibited some time previous by the whole of the inhabitants. In consequence of this, a force consisting of part of the garrison of the English fort, and a company of the militia, proceeded to intercept them on their return to the interior, but the troops could not be restrained, and having fired at a few of the Ashantees, who were in advance, the main body of them ran back into the Danish town.

On the morning of the 30th, another party of Ashantees arrived at Danish Accra for the like purpose, and the inhabitants expressing dissatisfaction at the measure, the Ashantees deliberately shot at a *mulatto* man coming out of the fort, and four other inhabitants who were unarmed: on this the whole of the town's people flew to arms, and killed fourteen Ashantees; some of them ran into the house of one of the traders, with whom they had been accustomed to deal, and others secreted themselves amongst the bushes, or among those whom they considered to be their friends. A short time after, the Ashantees attempting to make their escape, were attacked, when forty of them were killed, and a considerable booty fell into the hands of the Accras. The menaces of the inhabitants of Danish Accra induced Mr. Richter to apply to the British for an escort to bring those who had fled into his house, to the English fort for safety; but this request could not be complied with, unless application had been made to higher authority, and Mr. Richter was obliged at last to deliver them up to the people, who brought twenty-four Ashantees and five Fantee smugglers as prisoners to the English commandant, Captain Blencarne, of the Royal African corps, and requested that he would convey them to Cape Coast.

Sir Charles MacCarthy having organized a militia at Cape Coast, Annamaboe, and Accra, composed of the most intelligent natives residing in those towns, and being assured of the sincerity of the numerous native chiefs, including the Fantees who had arrived from different parts of the interior and along the coast, and who unanimously took the oath of allegiance to the British Government; trusting to the professions which had been made to them for protection, His Excellency sailed for the Gambia on the 17th, of May, in the *Cyrene*, to inspect the settlement of Bathurst, established by him six years previously on the island of St. Mary's, which was then a barren spot, but his fostering and beneficent measures had in a short time raised it beyond the most sanguine expectation to an astonishing state of prosperity. At a late hour on the 11th of July, he landed at Sierra Leone, with the officers of his suite. Brigade Major Ricketts, and Ensign Wetherill, 2nd West India regiment, private secretary, from the *Cyrene*, having sailed from the Gambia in eight days.

On his arrival he learnt that several of the native chiefs, both inland and near to the colony, were at war, and that trade was consequently stopped. He was also informed that Amorah, King of the Mandingo country, a powerful chief, had assembled a large force, and assisted by the Soolimas, a tribe some hundred miles in the interior, threatened to attack Dallah Mahamadoo, a chief residing on the Bullum shore, seven miles across from Freetown; being desirous of preventing the approach of hostilities so near to the colony, as well as of restoring trade. Sir Charles went himself in August, during the height of the rainy season, over to Dallah Mahamadoo, and having induced that chief to promise to be friendly with Amorah, should he be so inclined, sent Brigade-Major Ricketts and Lieutenant Austin, R. N. a few days after to Amorah on the Fouricaria River, one hundred miles distant from Sierra Leone.

They went in an open boat, and were two days and a night going up; their arrival was hailed by the people as the harbinger of peace and other blessings. Amorah was in camp near Fanghia, but he returned to Fouricaria to receive them. He promised to follow the advice of the governor; and on the return of the mission to Sierra Leone several gold and other merchants came at the same time in canoes from that country. The following anecdote is worthy of being inserted: on the mission taking their leave of Amorah, he, after disclaiming in a violent manner any animosity against Sierra Leone, which he had been accused of by his foes, said in broken English, "Dallah Moody bad man too much, he no king, he give me bad names, he call himself Englishman, and he say me Spaniard, me Portuguese, tell MacCarthy me governor like him, me Englishman."

Amorah is a very clever man: he writes Arabic well. The town of Fouricaria is extensive, and the houses neatly built; they appear like so many cottages at a good distance from each other. There were several Arabic schools in the town. The banks of the river are beautiful, and a good sized vessel can get up the river as far as King Amorah's town. Horses with country-made saddles and bridles were always ready for the officers of the mission, who rode about the country, which was beautiful and well cultivated with rice. The coffee tree grows wild here.

The mission returned to Sierra Leone after an absence of seven days. Brigade-major Ricketts having been desired by Sir Charles MacCarthy to hasten his departure, as he only waited his return to proceed to the Gold Coast, having received information that three thousand Ashantees had shewn themselves in the Fantee country on the 4th of June, and that Major Chisholm, who was in command there, had on the 11th sent Captain Laing with a large force of regulars, militia, and allies to meet them; the report of the advance of this force under Captain Laing induced the Ashantees to recross the Bosempra and return to Coomassie. The attention of Captain Laing was then directed to Appea, a chief of Adjumacon, being the only man of consequence in the Fantee country who had objected to take part against the Ashantees. The movement of Captain Laing's force to Ahmein, the residence of the King of the Fantees, induced that chief to join him with twelve hundred armed men.

The reason which prevented Appea from joining before was ascertained to have been a wish to learn the real intentions of the English, and not from a desire to support the Ashantees. After his junction, Captain Laing advanced to Adjumacon, Appea's country, and made preparations to attack Quashie Ahmonquah, a Fantee chief who had taken part with the Ashantees, and who was watching the actions of Appea: however Quashie Ahmonquah did not risk an engagement, but fled to the banks of the Pra, where he remained for a short time. Essecoomah, the capital of this chief, was destroyed by order of Captain Laing, who after that event returned to Cape Coast Castle.

About the 28th of July it was reported at Cape Coast that a body of Ashantees had entered the Fantee country with orders from their king to force their way to the Dutch settlement of Elmina: on receiving this information, Captain Laing was directed by Major Chisholm to march against them, it having been understood that they were approaching in the direction of Donquah when the sergeant was killed. At this place the force under Captain Laing remained for some time, and on its being ascertained by scouts that there was no probability of an immediate attack, Captain Laing was desired to leave his force at Donquah, and to proceed to Elmina, where he succeeded in inducing the acting governor to promise strict neutrality, and that if any parties of the Ashantees should reach Elmina, he would turn them out of the town; and if they should not comply, the inhabitants of that place would compel them to quit it by force of arms.

At daylight in the morning of the 13th of August Quashie Ahmonquah was attacked by Appea, who in this affair took eighty prisoners; he had himself a narrow escape with about three hundred of his people. Captain Laing, who was now, (1831), at Yancoomasie, on receiving this information dispatched a force to cut off his retreat. On the evening of the 18th Appea sent a messenger express to Yancoomasie, stating that the Ashantees were advancing in great force against him; upon which Captain Laing early next morning marched to his assistance with a detachment of the 2nd West India regiment, in company with the Annamaboe militia, and a party of the allies, who arrived at Adjumacon on the 20th, after a long and fatiguing march, and next day proceeded for Essecoomah, from which place Appea's advanced guard had been driven back that morning with the loss of one captain and six men killed.

The appearance of the troops caused the enemy to abandon the place in great disorder and without any resistance: they with their accustomed cruelty massacred the unfortunate prisoners who had fallen into their hands, whose bodies were found still reeking from the knives of their murderers. The near approach of night prevented the troops from pursuing them; and having halted until morning, they marched to the westward in search of the enemy, in which direction it was conceived they would fall in with them.

The attack was planned in five divisions, and they came upon the camp unobserved, which was immediately deserted by the enemy, leaving their dinners on the fire, their apparel, swords, knives, and among the rest some pillows of the leaders. The native chiefs were unwilling to follow up the enemy, from the excessive fatigue they had undergone, or it is supposed great advantages might have been the result, as Captain Hutchinson, of the Annamaboe militia, had been stationed with the Braffoes and Accoomfees, &c. at Monsue, where the retreat of the enemy might have been cut off, and forced to cross the Pra under a heavy fire. It was supposed this camp contained at least six thousand souls, but the natives said that the army, composed of Ashantees, Assins, and Quashie Ahmonquah people, was far beyond that number.

As the force of the Ashantees had not been correctly ascertained, Captain Blencarne, of the African corps, was ordered by Major Chisholm from Accra with a reinforcement to assist Captain Laing's division if required. Sixteen hundred men were ready immediately after the order was known; among the rest a company of the Danish Accras, accompanied by Mr. Richter, and Captain Bannerman, who commanded the militia, which were in a tolerable state of discipline. The Ashantees having retreated, Captain Laing returned with his forces to Monsue, where Captains Hutchinson and Fraser of the militia had been left in command of the main part of the Fantee Army. Another camp had been formed by order of Major Chisholm at D'Jouquah, distant inland from Cape Coast about eighteen miles to the north-west, composed of a party of the regulars, Cape Coast militia, and some of the allied forces, under the command of Lieutenant King, R.N. to prevent the Ashantees getting to Elmina and being supplied with ammunition from thence.

CHAPTER 3

Active Preparations for War

Sir Charles MacCarthy sailed from Sierra Leone on the 28th of October, in the colonial schooner, and arrived at Cape Coast on the 28th of November, having been thirty-one days on his passage from calms. On his landing, every countenance, black as well as white, expressed that joy which can only be compared to that produced in a family on the return of an affectionate parent. Soon after His Excellency's arrival, he visited the camp of D'Jouquah, then commanded by Lieutenant Mac Lean, of the Royal African colonial corps; and on his return proceeded, on the 15th of December, to Annamaboe. On landing, the crowd of chiefs, *pynins*, (a kind of magistrate among the natives,) men, women, and children, was innumerable; the air resounded with cries of "*Accoa ha E'woora O!*" meaning, how do you do master. His Excellency, after a short visit to the fort, inspected the militia. The parade here was also crowded by an immense population. After the inspection, the native chiefs with their martial bands, armed followers, dignitaries, and favourite wives, passed in succession before him, being seated under a neat bamboo hut erected on the ground for the occasion, surrounded by his suite, and the officers and gentlemen of Annamaboe.

The several chiefs shook hands most cordially with the governor, expressing in the strongest and most animated terms by words, countenance, and gesture, their satisfaction at his return among them. As soon as they had resumed their seats around the parade, their several officers marshalled their men, who went through the evolutions and firings of a sham fight; chief after chief sent his men, and various chiefs of towns situated at a small distance from Annamaboe, joined the meeting, their men taking a share in all the sports; the firings, &c. lasted for several hours; the reports of the muskets, the noise of the war drums and other instruments, the cries of the warriors, and the rejoicings of the women, produced such a singular effect, that it is impossible by words to depict an adequate idea of the scene.

The arrival of a messenger from Appea, king of Adjumacon, announcing his intended visit to Annamaboe to pay his respects to His Excellency, induced the governor to defer for another day his visit to the camp at Yancoomassie, in the Fantee country, which had also been formed in his absence by Captain Laing, under the directions of Major Chisholm.

On the morning fixed for the grand entry of Appea into Annamaboe, the whole line of the beach between that place and Agah, (one mile in length,) was crowded with the carriers of his army. As the day advanced, the line of dependants was succeeded by the armed men of this chief; innumerable umbrellas of various colours could be distinguished, and their glittering swords, with gold hilts, had a very imposing appearance. About eleven o'clock, notice being given of Appea's near approach, His Excellency left the fort, and took his seat in the bamboo hut before mentioned, everyhing indicating the rapturous ecstasy of the multitude; as Appea advanced, a dead stillness prevailed, which was only broken by the sudden sounds of horns and drums.

The procession, which entered the area in good order;, had been arranged with great taste, and the effect certainly exceeded expectation. Eight large canopies attracted curiosity from their ingenious construction of cloth of various colours, some of them diversified with figures; also some large umbrellas, carried over the several captains, riding in their *palanquins*, or litters of various descriptions, each captain or commander being surrounded by his own clan. At length Appea, of whom all had felt anxious to obtain a sight, appeared; he was carried by his own domestics, who, by every expression and attention, shewed their care of their master; he reclined on a satin cushion, with a handsome cloth of native manufacture, to cover his body if required; his *occras*, or confidential pages, preceded his *palanquin*, carrying elephants tails, emblematic of his power, and ten gold hilted swords; his first wife and sister were close in succession, followed by his bards, who sang his victories and great titles; his band followed playing their familiar airs, by which the deeds of their great men are recorded in the minds of the people.

His drums which played their part in the rehearsal of his power, were covered with tartan plaid, to hide the skulls and jawbones of his conquered enemies, with which they were decorated according to the custom of the native chiefs on this part of the coast; he being fearful, from the character he had heard of His Excellency, that they might give offence. As each of the chieftains of Appea drew near the bamboo hut, the captains alighted from their *palanquins*, and after making a low obeisance to His Excellency and uncovering both shoulders according to the custom of the country, they shook hands and endeavoured to evince every demonstration of respect and affection: each paraded to the spot allotted to him and his retinue: the same form was followed by Appea. The whole of the chieftains surrounded by their countrymen and adherents having taken their proper stations according to the custom of their country, the same compliment was observed by the *caboceers* of Annamaboe.

On the morning of the 20th of December, His Excellency, without any of those who were to accompany him, and without *palanquin* bearers, or anyone but a native guide, proceeded to Yancoomassie camp on foot, distant about twenty-seven miles in the interior of Annamaboe, and was seven miles off when his suite joined him. At the different villages through which Sir Charles passed to the camp, he was received by the women and children, who were the only persons left in them, with every demonstration of joy and respect, the men having all joined the camp. They sang songs in his praise, at the same time clapping their hands; some of the women offering him, and those who followed, palm wine and fruit, whilst others swept the street as he passed through their respective villages. They had never seen him before, but such fame had his goodness gained him, that he was looked upon as a supernatural being, which indeed his commanding stature did not tend to diminish.

On His Excellency's arrival at the camp, the native chiefs, ever ready to avail themselves of an opportunity to manifest their zeal, went through their evolutions. His Excellency was pleased with their attentions and expressed his wish to dispense with their firing; but Adookoo, King of Fantee, sent a polite message to him, saying he must do his duty whatever might happen, even if someone should be killed.

The whole of the native chiefs who joined in the rear against the Ashantees were not satisfied until they had evinced their sincerity by swearing allegiance in their fashion, as follows: the person about to swear took a sword in his right hand, and with great animation whilst expressing his determination called heaven to witness that he would be faithful to the cause, continually pointing the sword upwards at the governor's head, and flourishing it round his own, so near at times, that His Excellency's eyes were frequently in imminent danger. They would also swear on the bible, (white man's fetish as they termed it,) but before any of them would consent to join in the war against the Ashantees, Sir Charles was obliged to assure them, that he would never make peace with that tribe without acquainting them with his intentions, and that their interest should ever be considered.

The reason which they gave for making this stipulation was, that when, after a protracted defence, the Ashantee Army conquered the Assin country north of the River Bosempra in 1807, the resistance made by these people so exasperated the King of Ashantee, that he ordered every one who fell into his hands to be put to death. Those who could effect their escape sought safety by flight to Fantee. These unfortunate people, driven to despair, arrived at Cape Coast expecting to find protection, but on the contrary, the governor, Colonel Torrane, seized Cheboo their king, an old, infirm, and blind man, and delivered him over to the Ashantees, after they had arrived at Annamaboe, where he was put to death, with the most excruciating torture. Those of his people who had remained at Cape Coast with a hope that the life of their king would satisfy their enemies, were grievously deceived, for they were driven out by force, and harassed by every means that could be devised. Those who were taken prisoners and brought in, lingered out a painful existence in the dungeons of the castle, many of them died, and the few that remained were brought to the hammer and sold as slaves to the best bidder.

At Annamaboe, the treatment of the natives was equally dreadful; even those who had found protection in the fort were claimed by Colonel Torrane, on the pretence that the King of Ashantee had made a present of them to him; and many of them were actually sold, and put on board of slave vessels, others were transported to Cape Coast, where such scenes of human misery and suffering presented themselves as are too shocking for recital.

At His Excellency's arrival at Yancoomassie camp, there were several Assin chiefs, allies of the Ashantees, who had been waiting his arrival; these expressed a great desire to join him, and asked for fifteen days to make arrangements. They begged that the governor would allow the Fantees to let them have a little salt, which was granted to the extent of half a *tacoe*, in value equal to three pence half-penny, for this they were very thankful: on the 21st His Excellency visited Mac-Carthy Camp, a mile in advance of Yancoomassie: the surrounding country is beautiful. He called on his return at Donquah, where he was shewn the house in which the unfortunate sergeant was kept a prisoner and the large tree under which he was murdered. A child ten years of age, the son of the chief Paintry (the person alluded to in the Moorie affair) of that village was made a principal actor in that horrid scene, and was afterwards at school at Annamaboe.

The town of Donquah is very pretty; the main street is about sixty feet wide, with a row of trees in the centre, affording a beautiful shady canopy. The cross streets branch off at right angles. His Excellency walked the greater part of the way both going to and coming from Yancoomassie. Night approaching on his return, and the path being very rugged and dangerous, he was preceded by natives with *flambeaux*, the track being slippery, and from the quantity of rain that had fallen, they were sometimes up to their knees in water, and did not arrive at Annamaboe until eleven o'clock at night. The next morning early, His Excellency left that place for Cape Coast with the intention of proceeding to Accra, for the purpose of viewing the camp which had been formed in his absence, under the orders of Captain Blencarne of the Royal African corps.

On the 25th he inspected his regiment, the Royal African Colonial corps; and after a suitable address on the occasion to the European soldiers who had lately joined the regiment, on their duty as men and soldiers, exhorted them to support the character and honour of their country, not by bravery alone, but by a strict adherence to justice and humanity. To the native African soldiers he expressed his satisfaction at their general good conduct. His Excellency then presented to the regiment a handsome pair of colours.

In consequence of various accounts received through some of the native chiefs, our allies, respecting the movements of the Ashantees, one of which was that they were rapidly advancing to the coast in twelve divisions, His Excellency altered his intention of going to Accra, and directed Captain Blencarne to move forwards towards them with his division, in order to threaten the Ashantees in that quarter. Captain Laing was at the same time ordered to advance with the Fantee troops to the Assin country, with a view to make a diversion on that side; he himself proceeding to D'Jouquah camp, eighteen miles march, on the 29th, taking with him (with the exception of a few men and an officer left in the castle) the whole of the troops, consisting of the Royal African Colonial corps, a small detachment of the 2nd West India regiment, having marched on the 27th, and the militia, under their respective officers, on the 28th, for that place.

It would be difficult to describe the feelings of the native population on the departure of these troops to wage war against the tyrant who had so long been the scourge of a considerable portion of western Africa. On His Excellency's reaching the camp, the troops, including the native allies, were drawn up ready to receive him, and the natives greeted him in a manner far beyond any thing that can be conceived. He expressed great admiration and satisfaction at the appearance of so many fine men ready to avenge the murder of a British sergeant, who had shewn the Ashantees a specimen of the British character in denying to his last moment that their king was his master.

During Sir Charles MacCarthy's stay at D'Jouquah he was indefatigibly engaged, both morning and evening, in personally drilling the men to the bugle sounds and bush fighting. On the 4th of January a force of nearly two thousand men having been collected, a movement to Ampensasue, the headquarters of Annimelle, the King of Wassaw, on the left bank of the River Bosempra was determined on, and Major Chisholm, who had been left at Cape Coast to make some necessary preparations, was ordered to join the army on that day. The difficulty of procuring provisions and shelter on the rout, rendered it necessary to advance in small parties, which, together with the impossibility of obtaining carriers, retarded for some days the departure of His Excellency from the camp.

On the 8th of January, information was received of the entrance of the enemy into Western Wassaw, and that the allied forces in that direction were precipitately retreating before them; this information immediately decided the departure of His Excellency for the right bank of the river Pra, with such part of the forces that had not already marched for Ampensasue, and he directed Major Chisholm to proceed to assume the command of the latter place, signifying it to be his intention to send him instructions how to act, on ascertaining the state of affairs at Wassaw. The native chiefs at D'Jouquah, among whom were those of Cape Coast, on hearing of Sir Charles MacCarthy's intention of proceeding himself farther into the country, entreated of him to return to Cape Coast, stating that they did not think it becoming in their governor to command in the field against the Ashantees, unless headed by their king in person.

It had been said that it was the intention of Sir Charles to proceed to Coomassie, but the author does not think he was really serious, if he had ever entertained such an idea. It was evidently good policy in getting the surrounding tribes to join in repelling the enemy, otherwise they would have been forced to join the king, and those residing under our protection must have suffered, even if they had only their provision-grounds, and villages destroyed, which took place afterwards in the advance of the Ashantees to Cape Coast, and thousands of unfortunate beings would have been shipped off into slavery.

Sir Charles's movement into the Wassaw country, was to encourage the natives by his own presence and example in defence of their wives, children, and property; for the natives at this time dreaded even the name of the Ashantees, from the cruelties and impositions practised on them by that tribe.

His Excellency, on the morning of the 9th, proceeded on from D'Jouquah on foot for Bansoo, a village seventeen miles from that place, leaving a company of eighty men, natives of the Gold Coast, who had not long been enlisted for the Royal African colonial corps, commanded by Ensign Erskine, three companies of native militia, officered by the merchants of Cape Coast, consisting of one hundred and seventy men, who had not been long embodied, and about two hundred and forty unorganised natives, under their own captains, to follow him. The troops overtook Sir Charles half way, but the roads were so bad, that they did not arrive at Bansoo until late in the evening, much fatigued. They remained at this village the whole of the next day, waiting for the native force to come up, but which did not join them until late in the day.

On the next morning His Excellency, with the whole of the troops and natives, moved on for Heman, a village on the banks of the River Bosempra, leaving Brigade-Major Ricketts with the rear guard to see every thing forwarded: this he found great difficulty in accomplishing, as the carriers who brought the baggage from D'Jouquah camp had run away. Sir Charles would not consent to pay the natives the exorbitant price they demanded as carriers, and they entertained an idea that they would be looked upon by their countrymen as cowards, if they had not a musket, and did not join their clan. It was, in consequence, frequently impossible to procure carriers, and the brigade-major was obliged to impress women, as well as men, into that service, and to force them along with the baggage; but who, on finding a favourable opportunity, threw their loads into the woods, and disappeared.

On the morning of the 12th, His Excellency, with the troops, marched for Deraboassie, another village seventeen miles lower down, on the banks of the Bosempra. The path was extremely bad, having to climb precipices, and to pass through various swamps, frequently above the knee, and in consequence of which they did not arrive at Deraboassie until very late in the day, much fatigued; the native force, at the same time, kept a considerable distance in the rear.

At seven o'clock in the morning of the 13th, the troops commenced crossing the Bosempra in eight small canoes, which carried but two men at a time, besides the person who paddled, and as soon as the native company of the Royal African Colonial corps had crossed the river, His Excellency, who was one of the first that passed over, proceeded on with them for Assamacow, in the Wassaw country, distant about twenty miles from the river. This march was worse than any they had hitherto experienced, and they could only reach a small village that night, called Guah.

On the next morning, the 14th, His Excellency proceeded on with the men of the Royal African corps, desiring the militia to follow. The whole body of troops arrived at Assamacow at three o'clock in the afternoon, where they halted and remained five days, waiting for the native force to come up. During this period, an Ashantee girl and a lad arrived, who had been taken prisoners at some place near to Ashantee, and sent to Sir Charles. They stated, in reply to some questions that were put to them respecting the king, that when they left Coomassie, young virgins had been sacrificed on certain days in the week to the fetish for the recovery of his health.

The town of Assamacow is delightfully situated, and the houses have nearly the appearance of those in an English village of the better class. They are neatly built in a superior stile, and that in which Sir Charles MacCarthy was quartered, was ascended by a flight of twenty steps. The rooms are floored, and the windows have green jealousies; there was also a bedstead with curtains in his sleeping room. The houses are built of the same materials as those at Cape Coast, *viz.* swish and thatched roof. Mr. Brandon, the ordnance storekeeper, had arrived at this place a few days before by way of Sucoondee, which is situated on the sea coast, and whither he had gone by water with ammunition, which was much required, as the regulars and militia had only twenty rounds each, besides leaden slugs and loose powder, much of which had been damaged by the rain that had fallen on the march, in crossing the river and various rivulets, together with the want of proper means of security.

During the stay at Assamacow, Sir Charles was informed that the Wassaws and Dinkeras were retreating before the Ashantees, and were in want of provisions; he therefore, immediately on the arrival of the native force, dispatched Mr. Williams, the colonial secretary and adjutant general of militia, (who had been sent previously to Sir Charles's departure from Cape Coast, to report upon the state of this part of the country, and who had returned to D'Jouquah camp before His Excellency marched from thence,) to assure the Dinkeras and Wassaws, that he would in a few days join them, and that he expected the force under Major Chisholm, consisting of all the Europeans and most of the native men of the Royal African corps, the detachment of the 2nd West India regiment, and three companies of the militia, besides numerous parties of the allied forces, and which was, from the description of men of which it was composed, the main body of the army, to form a junction with him, he having written on the 17th, urging that officer to join him without delay.

Mr. Williams also received instructions to mark out a place for a camp, and to endeavour to get the Wassaws and Dinkeras to remain there until Sir Charles should arrive; but Mr. Williams found them in full retreat, and it was with much difficulty that he prevailed upon them to halt upon the banks of a small river called Adoomansoo, the spot which he had chosen for a camp.

On the morning of the 19th, in consequence of information from Mr. Williams, His Excellency dispatched Brigade-Major Ricketts at a few moments notice with the regulars and militia, to join him, desiring that a guard should be left for the ammunition, which would be forwarded under the care of Mr. Brandon, intending himself to follow with the native forces. The cries of the immense number of women and children, who had met together on the march, was most distressing, and there were some poor old men among them who tottered along on crutches.

Early in the day of the 20th, Brigade-Major Ricketts reached the river, twenty miles march from Assamacow, having been obliged to halt for the night in the woods exposed to heavy rains, the mud in some places reaching the troops above the middle of their bodies. Shortly after the brigade-major reached Mr. Williams with the troops, he was informed, that none of the natives would clear the jungle for the camp. The chiefs of the Wassaws and Dinkeras, on being told how necessary it was for a camp to be cleared, and that it ought to be begun immediately, promised to send people over to the opposite bank of the river, where it was supposed that the enemy would take up their position, to cut the wood down; but not long after this, the Wassaws mustered, and were decamping with every thing in their possession, and said they were going to clear the wood on the opposite bank of the river, the brigade-major stopped where they had to cross over, but at length it being plainly seen that their intention was to retreat, a strong guard of militia was posted to prevent them, until Sir Charles MacCarthy should arrive.

The headmen of the Wassaws were then sent for, and asked whether they intended to fight? to which they replied in the affirmative. At this moment an alarm was given that the Ashantees were advancing, and every one took his station, where they remained for about five hours exposed to a most tremendous storm of rain. It having now become dark, and it being a strict rule with the Ashantees never to fight at night, the troops were called in, leaving sentries where it was conceived necessary. Both officers and men slept this night without any covering, not having time to erect huts, and the men being much fatigued.

Immediately on the alarm being given, a messenger had been dispatched with the information to His Excellency, who was supposed to be at the time about five miles distant, who shortly returned with two letters, one addressed to the brigade-major, and the other to Mr. Williams, stating that Sir Charles did not believe it possible that the Ashantees could be so near, and attributed the alarm to a design of the natives to induce him to retreat, as some of their chiefs had, just before he left Assamacow, entreated him to recross the river Pra; he also added that he was determined to see how the Ashantees liked our balls.

On the next morning early, the 21st, His Excellency joined with about two hundred men from Appea, chief of Adjumacon, which he had sent as a bodyguard to Sir Charles, and forty natives of Cape Coast; the Commendas, amounting to several hundred, having halted on the way: he was also accompanied by Quashie Yacow, chief of Assamacow, an infirm old man, who was carried in a basket. Sir Charles did this to induce Quashie Yacow's people to follow him, they having shewn no inclination to move forward. His Excellency was informed of the manner in which the Wassaws had behaved, and after taking a little rest, (he being exceedingly fatigued, having come the whole distance from Assamacow on foot and having gone to reconnoitre the position that had been taken up) in the meanwhile he sent for the chiefs of the Wassaws and Dinkeras, and on his return and whilst he was yet in conference with them, the alarm was given, and every person repaired to his station. Sir Charles still doubting that the Ashantees could have advanced so near. His body guard of their own accord took up their position on the extreme left; Sir Charles missing them, sent repeatedly to desire they would come to him, but they positively refused, stating that they understood bush fighting and had got a position which they liked.

About two o'clock the enemy, who were said to be considerably more than ten thousand men, instead of being divided, as it was reported, were collected together, armed with muskets, and having a large description of knives stuck in their girdles, they were heard advancing through the woods with horns blowing and drums beating, and when they came within half a mile of our party they halted, when Sir Charles ordered the band of the Royal African corps which had accompanied him, to play "God save the King," and the bugles to sound, he having heard through some channel in which he placed confidence, that the greater part of the Ashantees only wanted an opportunity to come over to him. The Ashantees played in return, which was alternately repeated several times, and then a dead silence ensued, interrupted only by the fire of our men at the enemy, who had by this time lined the opposite bank of the river, which was here about sixty feet wide; having marched up in different divisions of Indian file through the woods with their horns, sounding the names or calls of their different chiefs: a black man who had been at Coomassie was able to name every Ashantee chief with the army, by the sound of their respective horns.

The action now commenced on both sides with determined vigour, and lasted till nearly dark. It was reported about four o'clock that our troops had expended all their ammunition, consisting of twenty rounds of ball cartridges, besides leaden slugs which were contained in small bags suspended by a sling round the men's necks, and loose powder contained in small kegs, carried also by the men themselves, application was made to Mr. Brandon, who arrived in the middle of the action, for a fresh supply of ammunition, he having received His Excellency's orders to have forty rounds of ball cartridges packed in kegs for each man ready to be issued. This was done to lighten the men, who had to carry respectively their own provisions for many days, as well as to preserve the ammunition from being damaged by the swamps and rain; but Mr. Brandon said that it had not yet arrived, and that he had only a barrel of powder and one of ball with him, which were immediately issued. He had left Assamacow with about forty natives carrying ammunition and was in advance of them when the engagement commenced.

The carriers who were natives of that and the adjoining countries, and who had been obtained at Assamacow more by persuasion than by any other means, seeing the Wassaws, their countrymen, making the best of their way from the battle, followed their example, nearly the whole of the guard it is supposed shared the same fate as most of their brethren the militia and soldiers: a corporal of the militia and one or two others, composing part of the escort, arrived at the place of action shortly before its conclusion, and reported that the carriers had refused to advance any further with the ammunition and that most of them had run away. On this circumstance being reported to Sir Charles, he desired to see Mr. Brandon, with whom he was exceedingly angry, and if he had not suddenly disappeared either into the woods or to look after the ammunition, it is probable that if Sir Charles had had the means at the moment, he would have put his threat into execution of suspending him to a tree.

The enemy perceiving that our fire had slackened, attempted to cross the river, which at this time had become fordable and succeeded. They had often attempted it when the river was swollen by the rains that had fallen, on trees which had been previously felled across to answer as bridges, but they were repulsed with great slaughter. The enemy had dispatched a considerable force to encompass our flanks in order to prevent our retreat, and now rushed in all directions on our gallant little force, who still defended themselves with their bayonets, until they were completely overpowered by their myriads, who instantly beheaded nearly every one of those who unfortunately fell into their remorseless hands. The Wassaws it appeared had left the field early in the action.

His Excellency, who had himself received several wounds, thus perceiving everything was lost on his side, retired to where Cudjoe Cheboo, the King of Dinkera, surrounded by his people, were bravely fighting. It is necessary to say something of this chief, as he will hereafter form a prominent character in this account of the Ashantee war. The late King of Ashantee suspecting that the King of Dinkera, who was at the time at Coomassie, had some intention of joining in the war against him, had him in consequence imprisoned, and Cheboo having received secret information through some female, that it was the intentions of the chiefs to put him to death, he by bribery communicated these circumstances to the people of his country, whose chiefs hastily assembled a strong party at Dinkera, and by concerted measures approached Coomassie, whence their king, Cudjoe Cheboo made his escape to them, and although the Ashantees, on the alarm being given, were alert in their endeavours to retake him, he escaped, and, on his arrival at Dinkera proclaimed war against Ashantee.

He sent some Ashantees who were then at Dinkera, working in the gold mines, to tell the new king that his captains were very trustworthy, as some of them had allowed him to escape for gold: on this the whole of the chiefs of Ashantee assembled, and after denying the accusation, unanimously swore on their most solemn oaths, which is by the head of their king, and Acromantie and Saturday, (see note following), that they would bring back to Coomassie the King of Dinkera or his head, should he even find protection within the walls of Cape Coast Castle. A large force being in consequence assembled, went in pursuit of him, who was joined by the King of Tueful, Awoosooco, as he passed through that country for Wassaw, followed closely by the Ashantee Army.

✶✶✶✶✶✶

Note:—About the year 1718, the then King of Dinkera (a young prince) sent some of his wives to compliment the King of Ashantee on some particular occasion. The king treated them kindly, and some time after sent some of his wives to return the compliment to the King of Dinkera and to assure him of his esteem. They were well received at Dinkera, but the king taking a fancy to one of them, prevailed on her to comply with his wishes, she departed afterwards with the rest for their country. The King of Ashantee becoming acquainted with what had taken place, assembled an army and engaged the Dinkeras, whom he defeated. The Akims having aided the Dinkeras, the Ashantees entered the country, and the king on his way to join them was suddenly attacked by a stronger party of the enemy than his escort, as he was crossing the River Pra and was killed, and nearly the whole of his followers shared the same fate. The war in consequence broke out with greater fury, and a town called Acromantie, in which the enemy had lodged the night previous to the attack, was burnt and totally destroyed and every living creature found in it put to death, hence the expressions "*Ioro Acromantie and Saturday*," (*Acromantie Meminda*) by which this calamity of Ashantee is remembered and which is prescribed by the laws as a most sacred oath of that country.

✶✶✶✶✶✶

Sir Charles, in joining the King of Dinkera, wished the men to be informed of his intention to retreat, but neither bugles nor any other instruments were to be had to give the requisite signal, every man of the African corps having joined his company in the action; and it was impossible, from the thick underwood where the men were now overpowered by the enemy and dispersed, to see many yards around, and a few wounded men only were got together.

A small brass field piece, which had arrived during the engagement, and flung down in haste, for it was still lashed with ropes to the poles on which it had been brought on men's shoulders, was about this time unloosed and the muzzle raised, whilst Mr. De Graft, a man of colour, linguist at Cape Coast and lieutenant in the militia, went round and obtained some powder from the King of Dinkera, with which and some loose musket balls, that had been left in a keg, it was loaded and fired in the direction of the enemy, in hopes to impede, in some measure, their advance; but they immediately afterwards rushed forward, and killed and wounded two men of the 2nd royal West India regiment, *viz.* the brigade-major's and Sir Charles MacCarthy's orderlies.

The brigade-major, who had been wounded, finding that His Excellency had left the King of Dinkera, followed in the direction which he understood he had taken, and shortly after observed him in a track in advance. He recognised him by his feathers. Soon after some musquetry was fired in front, and there was a general rush back of those who were with him, after which no more was seen of him. The brigade-major, followed by some of the wounded and Mr. De Graft, entered the thickest part of the wood, inclining towards the King of Dinkera, who still kept up a fire and retreating at the same time. A Wassaw man rushing by at this time, was fortunately seized by a militia sergeant who spoke the same language, and the man promised, if he was rewarded, that he would guide them through the woods.

A silver whistle and chain were then given to him by Mr. De Graft, on which he led the way, one of the party holding him fast. He took them first along side a stream of water, then out, and along the banks for a short distance; then in again and out on the other side, this he said was to conceal their track. The enemy at this time was close to them, scouring the woods, and they were obliged now and then to hide themselves.

It having at last become so dark that they could not see one another, the Wassaw man said that it was impossible to proceed until the moon arose; consequently they were obliged to halt for several hours. The rejoicing of the Ashantees on their success, and their attempt to sound some of the instruments of the band which they had taken, was distinctly heard, not being distant half a mile. About midnight the moon appeared, and the Wassaw man commenced cutting in that direction, the others following him; and when it began to descend, he halted, and said he could not proceed, until the sun arose, when he renewed his labour and continued until three o'clock in the afternoon, at which time they got into a track leading to Assamacow; and after proceeding a considerable distance, a party of the enemy was observed near to them; they therefore retraced their steps, till observing a small track to their right, which they took, the Wassaw man having decamped. This path led them into another, along which they had gone but a short way, when they met with about fifty Wassaws, who reported that there were Ashantees a little farther on.

Upon being asked where they were going, they replied in search of their families, whom the enemy had taken from their villages. Captain Ricketts then requested that he and his companions in arms might be allowed to accompany them, as it appeared that they intended to proceed in the direction where the division of the army under Major Chisholm would most probably be found. This proposal having been consented to, under a promise of reward, and it being near dark, the whole filed into the woods, and got on a small island surrounded with a swamp, in the crossing of which Captain Ricketts unfortunately lost his shoes. About one o'clock there was an alarm of the enemy having discovered them, but it turned out to be only two stragglers of the Ashantees, who perceiving a light, were induced to approach, thinking they might be some of their own people. They were immediately seized, and they insisted for a long time that they were Dinkeras, but a few of that tribe happening to be with the Wassaws, they without hesitation pronounced them to be Ashantees; on which every knife was drawn, and after getting from these two unfortunate persons all the information they could give, they immediately cut their throats.

They then sounded their horns, and proceeded by another direction to the River Pra. About six o'clock they fell in with a party of the enemy, and a kind of running fight ensued, and many of them were killed. The Wassaws recovered several of their wives and many of their children were found in the woods, some of the young infants in a dying state, and others with their brains dashed out, the Ashantees having obliged the women to throw away their children in order to enable them to carry their plunder. At last the whole party arrived at a deserted village on the banks of the Pra, where they were obliged to halt for the night, there being only a small broken canoe, that could scarcely swim, with which to cross the river.

Next morning at daylight, after the women had passed over, Captain Ricketts followed, but on being landed on the opposite side, he was so much exhausted that he could not move. Not long after, two European soldiers of the African corps having made their appearance, Captain Ricketts asked them if they knew him, to which they answered in the negative; but on telling them who he was, they, after looking for sometime with astonishment, recognized him, and took him up and carried him alternately on their backs to a small *croom* a few miles off, from whence they had come, and where they had left the remainder of the troops which had been sent in advance by Major Chisholm to prepare the natives to join him as he came along.

These poor fellows did all in their power to make Captain Ricketts comfortable; and having acquainted him that Major Chisholm was on the march to join Sir Charles MacCarthy, he expressed a wish to see him as soon as possible: the soldiers therefore constructed a kind of basket, in which they placed him, and having by force obtained a guide to shew the nearest way, took him up on their heads and proceeded; but after going some distance, through jungles and trees, the branches of which were at times obliged to be cut to allow the basket on the men's heads to pass, the guide said he could not find the path; they therefore returned to the *croom* with him, when he dispatched some of the black soldiers in another direction to meet Major Chisholm, who not long after arrived on the other side of the river, and who hearing of the captain's state, sent him clothes and provisions, following himself soon after.

Chapter 4

Captain Ricketts Takes Charge of the Army

It appeared that Major Chisholm had not received Sir Charles MacCarthy's letter of the 17th until the 22nd, and that another written by Sir Charles on the 21st, came to hand two hours before the former. It contained most pressing orders for Major Chisholm to join with his division immediately. The letter of the 17th had been unfortunately entrusted to a man unacquainted with the country, and was thus delayed three days. From this circumstance, and the urgent nature of the commands to join, and Major Chisholm fearing his consequent non-arrival according to His Excellency's most reasonable expectations would seriously derange his plans, proceeded by a shorter but unfrequented bad path, and having to cross the river Pra, at the distance of five miles from Ampensasue, on the 23rd, the whole day was consumed in passing his party over in a small canoe, and he was therefore under the necessity of halting for the night at a village on the opposite bank of the river, where he first received information of an engagement having taken place, but could not learn the result.

On the 24th, Major Chisholm had advanced twenty-one miles, when he received information that Brigade-Major Ricketts was lying wounded at an adjacent village. Major Chisholm had almost daily correspondence with Sir Charles MacCarthy, from the time of his leaving D'Jouquah on the 9th, until the 16th,. but the contents were chiefly comments upon the advance of his division, and the feelings of our allies towards us in the country recently passed through. Major Chisholm having ascertained the disastrous issue of the action of the 21st, and that his party was inadequate to cope with the immense force of the enemy, and also that it was impossible to afford any assistance to the party of Sir Charles MacCarthy from their complete dispersion, and being apprehensive that the Ashantees, flushed with their recent victory, would advance upon Cape Coast by rapid marches, he determined upon retiring thither.

They remained at this village until next morning, as all the men had not crossed the river till late in the evening, being obliged to construct rafts of any thing that could be procured. A great quantity of arms and ammunition were lost in the river, from the frail materials of which the rafts were composed.

On the 25th, Major Chisholm proceeded with his party to Cape Coast; Captain Ricketts being carried in a basket on the heads of some of the native soldiers, having a man in front with a cutlass to cut the wild vines and branches of trees; and the wounded men, blacks, were assisted along by their comrades. Not more than an hour after the march had begun, Captain L'Estrange, of the Royal African corps, who had gone in advance with his company, died from excessive fatigue. The troops halted for the night at a deserted village, and moved forward at daylight for Affettue, where they arrived at one o'clock in the day; and after a little rest, proceeded on for Cape Coast, which place they reached late in the evening.

Captain Laing, who, agreeably to his instructions, had advanced about thirty miles from Yancoomassie towards the Assin country, had arrived at Cape Coast with a considerable portion of his division, being the most numerous party of our forces, consisting of Fantees, a few regulars of the Annamaboe militia, and of some unorganised natives of the town, he having received from the officer in temporary command at Cape Coast, intelligence of the result of the action of the 21st, which he obtained from some of the wounded who had found their way to English Sucoondee, and were afterwards conveyed to Cape Coast in canoes, and in the colonial schooner. Every exertion was made to assemble a force sufficient to oppose the advance of the enemy, but the effect which Sir Charles MacCarthy's unfortunate action produced on some of the native allies was so great, that they made many excuses to avoid taking the field with the few remaining troops, as they expected an attack upon their own country, and said they could not leave their wives and children unprotected. However, Captain Laing, on the 5th of February, marched from Cape Coast for D'Jouquah with a detachment of the Royal African corps, followed by a small party of the Annamaboes and Fantees, in all about four hundred men.

On the 14th of February a force of about one thousand men having been collected, Major Chisholm ordered Captain Laing to move from D'Jouquah with his force to Commenda, where the major joined on the 15th, having determined to chastise the natives of Dutch Sucoondee for an insult to Captain Woolcomb commanding His Majesty's ship the *Owen Glendower*, and two of his officers on the 25th of January. These officers had gone on shore for the purpose of viewing the place, and in the expectation of having some account of the action, which they understood had taken place, when they were assailed by a large party of the natives, who pursued them with drawn knives to their boats.

The captain immediately went on board and returned with a party of marines, thinking that by alarming them, they might be deterred from offering such insults in future, but was much surprised to find his landing opposed by a large armed force: he nevertheless disembarked, and proceeded towards the town, amidst a discharge of musketry from the natives, which was returned with ample interest by the gallant marines. Captain Woolcomb attempted to set fire to the town, but without effect, from the dampness of the thatch. In this skirmish two marines and a *kooman* were killed and several wounded.

Major Chisholm was further influenced to punish the natives of this, once extensive town for acts of hostilities committed by them upon our poor wounded fellows who found their way to the water side after the sanguinary battle of the 21st of January; accordingly at daylight on Monday morning the 16th of February, the embarkation of the combined troops commenced on board the *Owen Glendower*, and the Sierra Leone packet, which was completed at sunset, when His Majesty's ship *Bann* hove in sight, and both vessels, with the packet, commenced beating to windward.

It was hoped that the expedition would have reached Sucoondee that night, when the disembarkation might have taken place immediately, and probably a body of the Ashantees would have been captured; but the vessels, owing to strong winds and currents, did not reach their destination until three o'clock on Tuesday afternoon, when, on a disembarkation taking place, the whole of the inhabitants, together with a party of about four hundred Ashantees, fled from the town, which was instantly set on fire; by eight o'clock the town was completely ruined, and every valuable, as well as rum, powder, and stores of every description, either burnt or blown up.

The troops re-embarked on the same day, and early the next

morning the boats of his majesty's ship *Owen Glendower, Bann*, and *Swinger*, went up along the shore, skirmishing with the natives, and on their return the ships proceeded to Cape Coast, where they arrived in the evening, leaving his majesty's brig *Swinger* off Commenda. The Ashantees, notwithstanding their loss in the action of the 21st of January, which from corresponding accounts must have amounted to several thousands, and whose army was now ascertained to be fifteen thousand strong, had ever since continued stationary at Assamacow. It being rumoured that they were making preparations for advancing on the 1st of March, and a force not exceeding six thousand muskets having been collected, the Accra militia, under Captains Hanson and Bannerman marched with other natives of British Accra.

It was not considered prudent to hazard a general engagement, but to take up a position on the banks of the river Bosempra, in order to dispute the passage with the enemy. Captain Laing was entrusted with the command of this force; but after residing a few days with them at Commenda, he returned to Cape Coast unwell, and proceeded shortly after to England, taking with him the official dispatches.

Captain Ricketts, who was now scarcely able to move, having been dangerously ill of a fever and dysentery ever since his return to Cape Coast, was directed to proceed to the banks of the Pra, and take charge of the army, until Captain Blencarne, who had been ordered up from Accra, should arrive. On Captain Ricketts' arrival at Commenda, conceiving that the Ashantees would probably cross at that part of the river which runs close to Chama, a Dutch settlement, he ordered such of the forces as had not yet proceeded to Deraboassie, Heman, and other villages along the banks of the Pra, to march for the mouth of that river, where they encamped. When the troops were drawn up in line, they made a formidable appearance, and could be distinctly seen by the enemy from Dutch Sucoondee, where many of them were stationed. The Accra chiefs sent over some of their fetish men, whom they thought would be safe as belonging to the same fetish as the King of Ashantee, but they were beheaded immediately. Frequent skirmishing occurred between these troops and parties of the enemy across the river at this place.

After Captain Ricketts had been here for some time, the native chiefs stationed in the villages along the banks of the Pra, sent to inform him that provisions were becoming very scarce, and they wished to cross the river and attack the enemy. The whole of the forces at this time had increased to nearly eight thousand men. They were told in reply, that the object was not to attack the enemy, but to prevent them from crossing the river; however they did not approve of this proposal, stating that the people were impatient for action, and would lose their courage if they waited much longer. The chiefs were then informed that as soon as carriers for the ammunition could be procured, the troops would join them; but every endeavour to procure carriers failed.

The native chiefs were then informed that if they did not furnish carriers for the ammunition, the troops could not join them, which after long palavers they reluctantly consented to. Captain Blencarne having joined. Captain Ricketts, received instructions from Major Chisholm, who was dangerously ill, to return to Cape Coast, as his services were required there; he accordingly delivered the command over to Captain Blencarne on the 10th of March, and repaired to Cape Coast, where, in consequence of the protracted indisposition of Major Chisholm, the discharge of the public duties of this critical period devolved upon him; and Major Chisholm, in his dispatch to the Colonial Office dated the 16th of March, 1824, was pleased to express himself in the following terms:

"In transmitting a copy of a report of the particulars of the action of the 21st of January, made to me by Captain Ricketts of the 2nd West India regiment and brigade-major to the forces, I deem it an act of justice to that officer to state that the late Sir Charles MacCarthy entertained a very high opinion of his zeal and merits, and that he had it in contemplation to bring his services to the favourable notice of his lordship; and also for the period of two years Captain Ricketts served under me at the time when commanding the 2nd West India regiment, in the capacity of adjutant and captain, I have pleasure in stating that I had every reason to be satisfied with his conduct; my protracted illness having incapacitated me from attending to the public duties, the charge in a great measure fell upon him as second in command, of which he acquitted himself entirely to my satisfaction."

Captain Blencarne, after much difficulty, having succeeded in getting the native chiefs to furnish carriers for the ammunition, left Chama camp early in the morning of the 12th to join the allied chiefs, Cudjoe Cheboo, Appea, &c. at Kemim, where he arrived at four o'clock in the afternoon. Great etiquette was observed in the entre of the Accra chiefs on the following day into the town.

Chapter 5

Advance of the Ashantees

About the 14th of March Governor Last, of His Netherland Majesty's settlements, who had lately arrived from Holland, wrote to inform Major Chisholm that some messengers had arrived at Elmina from the Ashantees, and that they wished a British officer to be present at a conference. The brigade-major accordingly went up and the Ashantee messengers with their resident ambassadors at Elmina, Achampong, and the principal natives of that place: having assembled in the castle, Governor Last desired them to state their business; accordingly they declared, that the King of Ashantee had not sent his army to fight with the white men, but to bring to him Cudjoe Cheboo, King of Dinkera, Awoosooco, chief of Tueful, and Annimelli, king of Western Wassaw, who had made war against him their sovereign; that if these three men were delivered up, the Ashantee army would immediately return home; but that they had orders from the king to take Cudjoe Cheboo in particular, although he should be locked up in Cape Coast Castle.

They moreover positively denied that the King of Ashantee gave orders to kill the sergeant, and said that the Fantees perpetrated that atrocious act of their own accord. Captain Ricketts told them that it was not the wish of the king of England to make war with any of the natives of Africa, but on the contrary to befriend them, and as a proof, pointed out the abolition of the slave trade; he added also that if the Ashantees were inclined to make peace, it could be effected at Elmina, provided proper persons were sent by them for that purpose. The Ashantee messengers then said they could do nothing in the business themselves, but would communicate what had been said to the chief of the army, and requested that orders might be given to our troops not to attack the Ashantees; they promising in the name of their army, that they would also remain quiet until some of their head men should arrive at Elmina for the purpose of endeavouring to make peace; orders were accordingly given to our troops to that effect on the 16th.

Governor Last having understood that Mr. Williams, the colonial secretary, who had been taken prisoner by the Ashantees, was still alive in their camp, desired the messengers to intimate to the chief of the army, that if he was regarded as a friend, they would best evince their sincerity by releasing Mr. Williams: he therefore sent them back in a canoe, with a trusty man and with some considerable presents for the Ashantees, *via* Chama. The messengers before leaving Elmina requested Mr. Last to obtain a letter to Lieutenant Scott, of the *Swinger*, at anchor off Commenda, not to molest any canoe going or coming from Chama, declaring that if the man of war attempted to stop any of those who might be bringing Mr. Williams to Elmina, they would immediately cut his throat.

About a week after, Mr. Williams was brought and delivered to the governor, after being first led through the town in a state of nudity, with his hands tied behind; and in giving him over to Mr. Last, they stipulated that he should not be allowed to go to Cape Coast or to any other place except Holland. With respect to the message concerning peace, they stated that the chiefs who had been appointed to meet at Elmina to negotiate, did not like to come by water, as they would be sea sick, but if our army should be withdrawn from the banks of the Pra, they would proceed by land; but this proposal not being acceded to, hostilities recommenced.

It appeared by Mr. Williams's statement, that he left the field of action in company with Sir Charles MacCarthy, Mr. Buckle, and ensign Wetherell, and, after proceeding a short distance along the track to Assamacow, they were suddenly attacked by a part of the enemy, who fired and broke one of Sir Charles's arms; and that he immediately after received another wound in the chest and fell. They then removed him under a tree, where all remained awaiting their fate, which they perceived to be inevitable.

Immediately after, Mr. Williams received a ball in his thigh, which rendered him senseless; previous however to his falling he saw Ensign Wetherell, who appeared also to have been wounded, lying close to Sir Charles, cutting with his sword at the enemy, as they were tearing the clothes off his friend and patron. Mr. Williams, upon recovering his senses, perceived that some Ashantees were attempting to cut off his head and had already inflicted one gash on the back of his neck;

luckily however, at this crisis an Ashantee of authority came up, and recognizing Mr. Williams, from whom he had received some kindness in the African company's time, withheld the hand of the savage: on Mr. Williams's recovering his senses, he saw the headless trunks of Sir Charles MacCarthy, Mr. Buckle, and Ensign Wetherell. He was then taken prisoner and marched to Assamacow, where the Ashantee Army was encamped.

During his captivity he was lodged under a thatched shed in the day time, and locked up at night in the same room with the heads of Sir Charles, Mr. Buckle, and Ensign Wetherell, which, owing to some peculiar process, were in a perfect state of preservation. Sir Charles MacCarthy's presented nearly the same appearance as when he was alive. Mr. Williams was only allowed for his daily food during his cruel confinement, as much snail soup in the morning and evening as could be contained in the palm of his hand. Whenever they beheaded any of their prisoners, they obliged Mr. Williams to sit on one side of the large war drum, while they decapitated the unfortunate captive on the other.

It was said that Mr. Jones, a merchant and captain of the militia, fell into their hands alive, and because he had received five wounds, he was sacrificed to the fetish. It seems that every person, whether Ashantee or prisoner, who may be so unlucky as to receive that number of wounds in one action, is considered as belonging to the fetish. It was also reported that Mr. Raydon, captain in the Cape Coast militia, was taken prisoner; that he was deprived of his clothes, and because he could not keep pace with them, they put him to death. It was the intention of the Ashantees to have sent Mr. Williams to Coomassie; but he not being able to walk that distance, the ball still remaining in his thigh, they endeavoured to extract it by tying the thigh tight with strings, both above and below the part where it was lodged, so as to force it out.

Mr. Williams declared that the pain was most excruciating; but not succeeding, he had reason to be apprehensive that they intended to put him to death, when the welcome intelligence of their intention to send him to Elmina was made known to him, after a captivity of two months. He reported that the discipline of the Ashantee Army, and the regularity with which the different duties were conducted, astonished him, and he added that the Ashantees estimated their loss in the action of the 21st of January to have been very great. The following are the names of the officers killed and wounded on the side of the British, in the battle near Assamacow.

Killed.

Brigadier-general Sir C. MacCarthy, Governor
2nd West India regiment: Ensign Wetherell, Dr. Tedlie, surgeon, J. S. Buckle, Esq., Colonial Engineer
Captain Heddle, Captain Jones, Captain Raydon, Captain Robertson, Merchants
Mr. Brandon, ordnance-keeper.

Wounded.

Captain Ricketts, 2nd West India regiment, major of brigade to the forces.
Ensign Erskine, Royal African colonial corps.
J. T. Williams, Esq., colonial secretary and adjutant general to the militia, (taken prisoner.)

About ninety of the soldiers and militia were wounded, many of whom subsequently died at Cape Coast from the hardships and privations which they had endured, and about one hundred and seventy-seven were killed, taken prisoners, or lost in the woods.

It having been erroneously reported to the allied chiefs that the English intended to give up Cheboo, and the other two chiefs before mentioned, to the Ashantees, in order to obtain peace, and the same having been apparently confirmed to them by Captain Blencarne having told them, (after he had given directions for the whole army to cross the Pra in order to attack the Ashantees, which they were making preparations for the next day,) that he had received instructions not to fire on the enemy until further orders, they immediately determined upon attacking the Ashantees themselves, and with that view, notwithstanding the endeavours of Captain Blencarne to dissuade them, they crossed the river on the morning of the 24th of March, about seven thousand strong, leaving him with the regulars, militia, and a party of Accras before-mentioned, in all six hundred men, and commenced cutting paths towards the enemy's camp.

Major Chisholm learning the mistake under which the allies laboured, sent Captain Hutchinson, of the Annamaboe militia, who volunteered his services, and to whom much credit is due for his zeal in the public service on every occasion, to undeceive them, by assuring them that the English would never consent to make peace on conditions of giving up those chiefs. Captain Hutchinson found the allies cutting their way towards the enemy, who it appeared were ignorant of their proceedings. He afterwards visited Captain Blencarne, who, with his force, had gone to the assistance of Lieutenant MacCarthy, of the 2nd West India regiment, who had been sent to Deraboassie to observe the motions of the enemy, and who reported that the Ashantees appeared in great force on the opposite bank of the river, and were endeavouring to cross over.

Skirmishes across the Pra between our troops and the enemy, occurred daily. One morning as Ensign Erskine, of the Royal African colonial corps, was sitting in a hut near the bank of the river, a ball from the enemy pierced the hut, and lodged in his thigh, which disabled him. The enemy got possession of all the ammunition, which, on account of the good accommodation it afforded, had been left at Assamacow, and burnt that village on leaving it. Eight days had now elapsed since the allies first commenced cutting paths to the Ashantee camp, situated half way between Assamacow and the River Pra, and they having acquainted Captain Blencarne that they had got near enough to the enemy, whom they intended to attack next day, that officer made arrangements for crossing over with his party to engage their right flank, as soon as he should hear the firing commence.

But after the allies had been nine days thus occupied, and enduring many privations, the chiefs of the right informed those on the left, composed principally of Wassaws, that they were ready to attack the enemy next day, when their courage failing them, being near the river, they crossed it at night, followed by the others. There being no other mode of conveyance, they swam over, supporting their firelocks on plantain stalks and branches of trees, and thereby lost two thousand stand of arms, with nearly all their ammunition, and several of the men themselves were drowned.

The attention of the Ashantee Army was now aroused by the noise made by the allies, who as they landed, dispersed in various directions, and made their way home, being nearly exhausted by hunger. Captain Blencarne finding himself thus left with only the regulars and militia, who were in as bad a condition as the allies, and in readiness to cross the river, gave orders on the morning of the 2nd of April, for his party to return by way of Affettue to Cape Coast, and some of them retired on Commenda fort, from whence they were conveyed in his majesty's brig Swinger, and the Sierra Leone packet, to Cape Coast. The embarkation took place in great haste, as it was said that the enemy was rapidly advancing on Commenda.

The enemy did not march to Commenda immediately after this, but occupied the camp on the banks of the Pra which our forces had quitted.

During the nine days that the allies were cutting their way to the enemy, the few officers who were with Captain Blencarne visited daily the different outposts along the banks of the river. Lieutenant Mends, of the Royal African corps, being the only officer present capable of fatigue, this arduous duty almost solely devolved upon him, and in the performance of it, he had frequent skirmishes with the enemy's foraging parties across the river. Many Wassaw women, who had been captured by the enemy, daily made their escape, and swam across the Pra to the troops: their appearance from cruel treatment and starvation, was truly wretched. On Captain Blencarne's way to Cape Coast, he fell in with the King of Dinkera at Bansoo, and endeavoured to persuade that chief to accompany him to Cape Coast, but without effect, until he had satisfied him that the English would never deliver him or any of his family to the King of Ashantee. The King of Dinkera's distrust of the British arose from the cruel act of delivering over the old chief of Assin, Cudjoe Cheboo, to the Ashantees.

On the 10th, Major Chisholm again ordered Captain Blencarne out with his troops to form a camp at Affettue, twelve miles from Cape Coast. He was followed by the King of Dinkera, and Appea, with their people, who, at the request of Captain Blencarne, took up a position near a village called Dompin, twelve miles in advance, and close to a stream of water from which the enemy obtained their supply. Cudjoe Cheboo having been joined by Appea and the other natives, determined on preventing the enemy from procuring water from this brook, and fired at several of them. Some of the Ashantees soon after called out that they would soon see who was master; accordingly, on the morning of the 25th of April, the enemy approached and attacked the allies, who fought bravely for a considerable time, and imagined that they had the advantage, but it was only a manoeuvre of the Ashantees, whose centre had retired a little in order to induce the allies to advance; upon which they wheeled upon their flanks to the right and the left; and such of the allies as escaped, sought safety by flight.

Amongst these was Appea, who having been thus separated from his men, and not being heard of for several days after the others had reached the Cape, parties were sent out with bugles, and some of his own men with their horns, to sound in the direction it was presumed most likely for him to have sought safety, should he have been fortunate enough to escape the enemy. After the lapse of many days, and when all hopes of him were nearly abandoned, he was discovered in a most miserable and emaciated condition, crawling in the direction of the sound of one of the horns. He was brought to Cape Coast, where he died soon after of the small pox; thus fell the chief of the Adjumacon country, whose fidelity remained to the last.

The troops of Affettue, on hearing the firing, marched to the assistance of the allies; but on ascertaining that the enemy were cutting paths in every direction towards Affettue, and that the allies had been defeated and dispersed, they, under these circumstances, found it necessary to fall back on Cape Coast. As the troops and allies were leaving Affettue in haste, at one end of the town, on their way to Cape Coast, the enemy were entering it at the other, and nearly made Ensign MacKenzie and some of the European soldiers prisoners. However, he escaped out of the window, and with some of his men, covered the retreat of the troops, and killed several of the enemy.

Shortly after the troops were again ordered out, and directed to encamp at the government garden, five miles from Cape Coast, and about the same distance from Affettue, where the enemy had fixed their quarters. After much difficulty in getting the natives to the camp, a force of about six thousand men, including regulars and militia, was collected, and it being reported that the King of Ashantee was rapidly advancing with ten thousand men to reinforce his army at Affettue, Major Chisholm ordered his men to cross the small river which runs close to the garden, and to commence cutting paths to the enemy's position.

Several days elapsed before the allies had agreed who were to take the right, which position the Fantees insisted on occupying; but the others, knowing the cowardice of this tribe, and that the way to their country lay in that direction, objected in the strongest manner to this arrangement, and wished the Fantees to be placed on our left, as by this means they could not easily run away, having the Elmina people (friends of the Ashantees) and the sea on their left: but the Fantees would not yield, and at last succeeded in carrying their point by saying, that if they were not allowed to take the right, they would return home without fighting. This being settled, and the army told off in divisions, each commenced cutting their own way to the enemy, now about four miles off, through the thick prickly bushes.

The disastrous result of the action of the 21st of January did not reach Sierra Leone until the 16th of April, in a letter from Brigade-Major Ricketts, by His Majesty's ship *Victor*. The melancholy intelligence of a beloved governor, the friend of mankind and the idol of every loyal and grateful heart within the colony of Sierra Leone, having fallen by the hands of savages, produced those feelings of sincere regret in the minds of the inhabitants which can be better conceived than described; as he possessed every quality calculated to secure the fidelity and attachment of all classes of people who had the happiness to be placed under his government.

Chapter 6

Engagement with the Ashantees

On the 27th of April Lieutenant-Colonel Sutherland sailed from Sierra Leone with troops in His Majesty's ship *Driver*, Captain Bowen, having a commission from the acting governor, Mr. Hamilton, to assume the civil government of the Gold Coast: he arrived at Cape Coast on the 18th of May, and on the 19th, proceeded with Major Chisholm to join the army, who were cutting paths to the enemy's encampment; but he not wishing to deprive Major Chisholm of the credit of the command in the action about to take place, returned to the castle to hasten the preparations, and to forward the necessary supplies. Every man whose health would permit was ordered to join the army, as the near approach of the King of Ashantee with a reinforcement rendered it desirable that the enemy at Affettue should be attacked if possible before a junction could be formed.

On the 21st the castle and towers were garrisoned with marines from the squadron; and Major Chisholm having, after great exertion and fatigue, succeeded in cutting paths to the enemy's position, the action commenced at one in the afternoon. They were on a height concealed by thick woods; and had cleared all the bush wood or jungle in the direction in which our army were advancing, so that they had a full view of the men as they formed into line, after having marched in divisions of Indian file through the paths, which they had cut: the Ashantees could only be seen at intervals, and when making attempts to turn our flanks; but finding themselves, after fighting bravely for five hours, baffled at all points, they ceased firing and retired, as it was afterwards ascertained, with great loss; whilst that on our side was comparatively small.

No officer was killed, and only one wounded, *viz*. Captain Hutchinson, of the Annamaboe militia, who received a ball through both

II Smith's Tower

Cape Coast

2. Phipps Tower

IV King Aggary's House   III Fort MacCarthy

Castle & town

wrists, while in the act of encouraging his men. The King of Dinkera, who was on the left flank, behaved with much gallantry, and followed the enemy into the town of Affettue. During the engagement he sent along the line a bowl containing six Ashantee heads, which was carried on the head of one of his people, who ran with it to Major Chisholm by his chief's order, to shew what he was doing. The Fantees, three thousand strong, as it was expected, ran off to their own country at the first volley without firing a shot.

It being now nearly dark, their troops having expended their ammunition, the carriers supposing that we were defeated from the Fantees running away, returned to Cape Coast with the supplies. The troops and allies being much distressed for water, of which there was none to be procured nearer than the government garden, retired to that place, intending to renew the engagement on the next day. They accordingly moved forward in the morning, and halted at a short distance, in expectation of being followed by the auxiliary forces; but with the exception of the King of Dinkera and a few of the Cape Coast natives, the whole dispersed. On Colonel Sutherland's receiving this intelligence, he ordered the troops into the castle, leaving a party of observation under Lieutenant Rogers of the Royal African corps at the garden.

The Ashantees returned to Affettue two days after, and on the 28th they were joined by the army under their king. It was said that part of his army was in the action, having arrived at the commencement, and that some of the principals in the murder of the sergeant, who had come with them, were killed. It was also reported and believed, that a strong party of Elminas had joined the enemy in the action. After this they continued for some time without any movement. All the prisoners taken at this time agreed in stating that Osai Tootoo Quamina, King of Ashantee, had died at Coomassie at the commencement of hostilities, and that Accatoo Osai, his brother and successor, had left Ashantee, accompanied with all the warriors he could muster, and was determined to destroy Cape Coast, and drive the English out of the country. Soon after the arrival of the new King of Ashantee at Affettue, he sent a fetish or sanctified boy to our advanced post at the garden, to tell the governor of Cape Coast that the walls of the castle were not high enough and should be made higher; and that he ought to land all the guns from the men of war, as he intended to throw every stone of the castle into the sea.

After about three weeks preparations, during which our scouts and small parties were very successful in cutting off the enemy's foraging stragglers, the above message was followed by the king's advance from Affettue on the 21st of June, with his whole army, to within five miles of the castle, driving in the party of observation stationed at garden village where our army had been encamped. On the 22nd the enemy moved considerably nearer to Cape Coast, and took up a line about three miles in extent; the bush was so thick that their strength could only be judged by the smoke of their fires. On the 23rd they advanced so near that they were distinctly seen in great force on the heights. An attack on Cape Coast was consequently momentarily expected, and the male inhabitants of the town were ordered to make all possible resistance.

The women and children, amounting to nearly five thousand, most of whom had been driven in from their respective towns and villages as the enemy had advanced, and others from *crooms* adjacent to Cape Coast, now rushed into the castle, and as only the wicket of the gate was left open, which admitted only one person at a time, the screaming of the children, the melancholy cries of the women squeezing for entrance, was beyond anything that can be conceived. The seamen and marines from His Majesty's ship *Victor*, and the merchant vessels in the roads, were landed to man the guns, and every other possible means used for defence.

The enemy appearing to have received some account of these proceedings when within much less than a mile from the castle, halted, and early on the morning of the 24th, retired to the government garden(our late camp) where they remained stationary to the end of the month, detaching strong parties to lay waste the country, and to burn and destroy all the circumjacent villages, which they effected with impunity, our garrison not amounting to more than three hundred and sixty men, one hundred and four of whom were in the hospital, exclusive of a few artificers and militia, besides a very small unorganised native force, on whom but little dependence could be placed.

On the report of the enemy's advance on the 22nd, Lieutenant-Colonel Sutherland ordered some houses which were very near, and overlooked the ramparts of the castle on the land side, to be pulled down, but his commands were not attended to by the townspeople, and the garrison were too weak to execute them. On the 23rd, when the officer. Captain Hutchinson, threw out a signal from Smith's tower, that the enemy were advancing from the westward, he ordered four of these houses to be set on fire, but owing to a sudden increase of wind, the flames extended farther than was anticipated or intended, and notwithstanding every exertion, burnt the grass-thatched roofs, and the doors and windows, of nearly every house in the town. In consequence of the previous removal of goods into the castle, the floors of the houses being chiefly composed of mud thickly plastered over strong laths, and the houses being built principally of swish or clay, not much property was destroyed.

His Majesty's ship *Thetis*, Captain Sir John Phillimore, arrived on the 4th of July from England with men and officers of the Royal African corps, who with his men subsequently rendered most effectual service, which it was supposed induced the enemy to recall their foraging parties and concentrate their army. On the 7th they were seen in great force defiling over a hill in several paths towards some heights which they had occupied. Near to the left the king pitched his tent, and the bush having been cleared about the spot, his movements could be plainly observed with a glass. Some of his men wore the uniforms of our officers and men who had been killed, or taken prisoners at Assamacow, they also displayed the English, Dutch, and Danish flags, with others of their own making. We were at this moment very badly supplied with ball, and were obliged to take all the water pipes from the castle, the lead from the tops of the merchants' houses, and all the pewter pots and pans that could be procured, the ships furnishing all the lead it was possible to spare, for the purpose of cutting up into slugs by the sailors, who were employed at this work for many days and nights both on board and on shore.

On the 6th a strong force of natives, consisting of about five thousand men from Accra and to the leeward of Cape Coast as far as the River Volta, having arrived, as well as some of the Fantees and other natives, who with the Cape Coast people having been supplied with arms and ammunition as well as our limited means would allow, a position on a commanding chain of heights opposite to the enemy was taken up on the 8th, from which time until the 11th the auxiliaries were employed in clearing away the bush in their front, and reconnoitring the movements of the Ashantees, with whom they had occasional skirmishing, and who were busily employed in cutting paths through the jungle to us.

On Sunday the 11th, soon after day-light, the enemy were descried in several strong masses descending the hills, and forming into lines in the valley, about half a mile from the town, between us and their former position on the heights. About two in the afternoon, the enemy's advanced party having been fired at by some of our skirmishers, commanded by Mr. Gordon, then a writer in the public service at Cape Coast, and afterwards an ensign in the African corps, a general engagement ensued, and continued until dark, when the enemy retired. Two of their camps, during the action, were burnt and plundered by some of the unorganised natives, who, although daily driven out of the town to their posts at the point of the bayonet, fought bravely this day for four hours, particularly those on the right, against which the greatest efforts of the enemy, who shewed great courage, were directed.

On the 12th, they again drew up in the valley, apparently with the intention of renewing the action; in order, however, to ascertain their object, some skirmishers were ordered to creep through the bush, fire at them, and retire, after which, the enemy's whole force returned the fire, and kept it up for half an hour. They made no movement afterwards until two in the afternoon, when a few random shots were fired from a field piece at them, through the bush, on which they retired to their former position. In the morning of the 13th, they were again observed in motion, descending in Indian files through several paths towards the valley, from the heights on which the king had pitched his marquee.

A renewal of the engagement was now momentarily expected by us, and we were accordingly prepared. They still continued marching down the hills until dark, when numerous fires were observed in the valleys; but when daylight appeared, not one of them could be seen, and it afterwards appeared by the statement of some of the natives on our side, who had been taken prisoners at Assamacow, and had made their escape from the enemy after this action, that it was a manoeuvre of the Ashantees to enable their women, wounded men, and carriers, to retreat unobserved; that they came down the hill on the side in our view, went through the bush to the other side, where they could not be seen by us, then ascended the hill, and came down again in front towards us.

As soon as it was known that the enemy had retreated, every effort was made to persuade the allies to follow them, but without effect. They had retired in the direction of the government garden, Elmina, and Affettue. A brother to Adookoo, king of the Fantees, who had been taken prisoner by the Ashantees, when they attacked and beat the Fantees in 1807, made his escape from the enemy on their retreat on the 13th, and stated that he was umbrella bearer to the king, and was with him in the action of the 11th. The Ashantee Army had suffered dreadfully from small pox, dysentery, and want of provisions, which had carried off many thousands, and, in consequence, caused so much discontent and insubordination in their army, that on the night of the 11th, whole bodies had deserted from the king, who were ascertained to be Assins, and who afterwards joined our native allies. He further stated, that the heart of Sir Charles MacCarthy was eaten by the principal chiefs of the Ashantee army, that they might imbibe his bravery; that his flesh had been dried, and with his bones, divided among every man of consequence in the army, who constantly carried his respective proportion about with him, as a charm to inspire him with courage.

Lieutenant-Colonel Grant, of the Royal African corps, having arrived from England on the 18th with ammunition, and a few men of the artillery and rocket corps, Lieutenant-Colonel Sutherland resigned the command to that officer, and returned to England in His Majesty's ship *Thetis*.

On the 19th, Lieutenant-Colonel Grant being informed that the enemy were encamped about six miles from Cape Coast, purchasing all their supplies from Elmina, sent out an auxiliary force to annoy them, which returned on the following day with several prisoners, and reported that the enemy had retreated in the direction of Annamaboe.

They remained in the Fantee country, destroying the villages and provision grounds, until they received intelligence that the Queen of Akim, who upon hearing of the defeat and death of Sir Charles MacCarthy, had sent one hundred men as a body guard to Major Chisholm, was about to invade their capital. The king hastily proceeded thither, leaving many hundreds of his sick and wounded behind, who fell into the hands of the Fantees, by whom they were nearly all beheaded.

When the Ashantees advanced from Affettue to the government garden, they sent out parties as far down as Annamaboe, which caused all the women and children of the different villages to seek protection at Cape Coast and Annamaboe fort. A famine, in consequence, soon ensued, which, in conjunction with the small pox and dysentery, carried off great numbers. Many were seen dead and dying in the streets, when the women and children were pent up in the castle, which they quitted on the arrival of the Accras. The scene was distressing; they were so crowded together that it was impossible to pass from one part of the yard to the other without walking upon them. The stench which they caused was horrible: it frequently rained, and a great deal of the filth and dirt created by them was washed into the tanks which contained the water used by the garrison. There is a large pond in the town, but the water is very unwholesome, and seldom or never used by Europeans.

The officers and soldiers were also very short of provisions, having neither meat nor flour, and but little rice. Five or six Europeans, including now and then an officer, died daily, from the excessive fatigue they had undergone, and want of proper food. If a supply of provisions had not providentially arrived from Sierra Leone, the result must have been truly disastrous. Several vessels also laden with rice, were dispatched from England as soon as the state of famine to which the natives were reduced was known, and by this timely supply alone they were preserved from perishing, as the enemy had destroyed every thing, and they themselves suffered much from the want of provisions.

The principal object of the advance of the Ashantee Army on the 21st of June so near to Cape Coast, was to get Cheboe, King of Dinkera, into their power. He was in consequence prevailed upon, with his sister, who had accompanied him from his country, to take up his quarters inside the castle, where, not long after, the latter died, and was buried in a spot of ground which he selected on the top of a hill, not far from the town.

A short time after Cheboe was observed by some native soldiers of the African corps, who were on picket close by, ascending the hill accompanied by a female: they in consequence watched their actions, knowing the custom of the inland tribes of sacrificing human beings over the grave, and that such practice was prohibited by the government of Cape Coast. They saw him approach the place where the remains of his relative had been interred, after which he bemoaned her loss, and shed tears to her memory, and was about to put the woman to death, who appeared perfectly resigned; when his intention was arrested by the soldiers, who escorted him back in company with the female to the castle, and on being asked his reason for this conduct, replied in a dejected tone, that the woman had been for a long time a faithful servant to his sister, who was very fond of her, and that she would be angry with him if he did not send her handmaid to attend upon her in the other world. The poor creature was kept for security in a room in the guard-house, until it was certain that Cheboe would not kill her.

After the action of the 11th of July, as some of the Commenda women and children were returning through Elmina to their homes, which had also been destroyed by the enemy, they were seized and beheaded by the natives of that town. Lieutenant-Colonel Grant, on hearing of this atrocity, wrote to Mr. Last, the governor of that place, on the subject; who replied that he had not sufficient means to control the ferocity of the people. Commodore Bullen being at anchor in Cape Coast roads at the same time, Lieutenant-Colonel Grant requested of him to allow one of the squadron to convey Brigade-Major Ricketts and Lieutenant A. C. Atchison to Elmina, for the purpose of offering Major Last the assistance of troops from Cape Coast Castle.

The *Victor*, Captain Woolcomb, was consequently appointed to convey those officers to Elmina. Major Last appeared thankful for the offer, and every arrangement was made, and the time fixed for the reception of the troops, at that place, but on the return of the officers to Cape Coast, Lieutenant-Colonel Grant received a letter from Major Last, stating that the natives of Elmina were determined not to allow any English soldiers to be landed there, which terminated the business. Had this object been effected, it would no doubt have put an immediate end to the war with the Ashantees, who obtained all their supplies from thence, and who were encouraged by the natives to persist in hostilities. Had the Elminas followed the example of the Danes, the Ashantees would never have come down to the coast in such a hostile manner.

CHAPTER 7

The General Departs for Sierra Leone

In formation having been received by Lieutenant-Colonel Grant, commanding the forces, that several of the officers had died at Sierra Leone, and that Captain Winter, the only officer of that rank, (who had been but a short time with the 2nd West India regiment) was obliged, in consequence of ill health, to return to England, and had died on his passage; Brigade-Major Ricketts was sent to take the command of the troops on that station.

He sailed on the 12th of September, 1824, in His Majesty's brig *Swinger*, the commander of which. Lieutenant Scott, died on the third day after departing from Cape Coast, of the yellow fever. This officer had rendered great assistance during the contest with the Ashantees in 1824; he also frequently landed the seamen and marines of his vessel, and often procured volunteers from the crews of the merchant ships in the roads to assist the garrison upon an attack being repeated.

Nothing worthy of particular notice occurred on the Gold Coast from this period, until the death of Lieutenant-Colonel Chisholm, which took place on the 17th of October. He had suffered a bad state of health for a considerable time, and was on the point of returning to Europe, after having served on the coast in various military capacities from the year 1809. He was unacquainted with his recent promotion. His unwearied assiduity and attention to his duties, his unceasing efforts to render happy all those whom Providence had placed under his care, had endeared him in a peculiar manner to the inhabitants of those regions, and rendered his loss a source of deep regret and poignant grief.

Major General Turner arrived at Cape Coast at the latter end of

March 1825. He was accompanied by three transports, having on board European soldiers of the Royal African corps, whom he had brought from England with him, and two hundred men of the 2nd West India regiment from Sierra Leone. His intentions in bringing such a force to the Gold Coast did not transpire, but he issued the following proclamation.

> By His Excellency Major-General Turner, C. B. captain-general and commander in chief of the British Settlements on the western coast of Africa:
>
> Charles Turner to the people of Cape Coast, to the people of the other British settlements on the Gold Coast, and to the surrounding nations, friends and allies of England: The king of the Ashantees has, by assistance of the Elmina people, waged a cruel and unjust war against you and us: he has suffered for his crimes and rashness, and Elmina is only suffered to stand because the king of the Dutch and the king of England, my master, are at peace; but I have represented their conduct, and their fate will depend on the orders I may receive. You have all stood forward in defence of your rights, and I thank you in the name of the king my master. England does not wish for any wars: she wishes the natives of Africa to be free, happy and rich; she wishes for nothing in this country but lawful trade and commerce. If the King of Ashantee will content himself with governing his own nation and his own people, and does not stop the trade of the interior with the coast, or attempt to oppress his neighbours, let him say so to me, and I will make a treaty with him on these terms; but I will not make peace with him on any other terms, nor until he gives up every claim to tribute or subjection from the surrounding nations.
>
> Given at Cape Coast this 2nd day of April, 1825.
>
> By His Excellency's command,
>
> William Williams,
> Acting Colonial Secretary.
>
> God save the King.

General Turner having made certain arrangements on the Gold Coast, where he remained only a short time, departed from thence on the 14th of April for Sierra Leone, with nearly all the European troops, and dispatched the transports with the detachment of the 2nd West India regiment on board for the West Indies. This distinguished officer died on the 7th of March, 1826, at Sierra Leone, having been but fifteen months on the coast. Upon this lamented event, Major General Sir Neil Campbell was appointed to the government, and colonel of the Royal African corps on the 18th of May 1826, and intelligence having arrived of the advance of the Ashantees to the coast again, in an hostile manner, he was ordered to proceed to Africa immediately; and he accordingly sailed from Portsmouth on the 22nd of July, in His Majesty's ship *Lively*, Captain Elliott, C. B. which had been appointed to take him out: he was accompanied by several officers of his regiment, and Captain Ricketts of the 2nd West India regiment, who had returned to England for the benefit of his health, and who was induced, from promises held out to him of promotion, to return to Africa, where he had previously served constantly for seven years.

Sir Neil Campbell arrived at Sierra Leone on the 22nd of August and sailed again in the *Lively*, early in September, for the Gold Coast. The *Lively* arrived in Cape Coast roads on the 19th of September, when His Excellency learnt that an action with the Ashantees had taken place. The spot where the battle was fought is a plain with small clumps of trees and underwood at intervals, about twenty-four miles north-east of British Accra, and nearly four miles south from a village called Dodowah, by which the natives distinguish the action. The King of Ashantee had pitched his tent there that morning. It was expected by every person who was acquainted with the Ashantee customs, that they would attack our lines on Monday, that being their prosperous day; accordingly some scouts brought intelligence about eight o'clock in the morning, that the enemy were in motion, and the king's drum was distinctly heard beating the war march.

Our line was in consequence formed with all possible expedition, extending about four miles east and west, which made a very picturesque appearance, from the various dresses and numerous flags, British, Danish, and Dutch, which waved in the air. Our men were decorated with large sea shells suspended from their necks and shoulders before and behind, or were decked with a stripe of white calico to distinguish them from the enemy. Many of fought with the cloth hanging from the barrels of their muskets, which added to the novelty and singularity of the scene.

A dispute had taken place for several days previously among the kings of Akimboo and Dinkera and the Queen of Akim, who should attack the King of Ashantee hand to hand; it was at last agreed, that the former should take up a position on our extreme right, and the

RA

two latter on our extreme left; but they were perhaps fortunately disappointed in this arrangement, as it was afterwards known that the King of Ashantee had received intelligence that there were white men in the camp, and in the centre, he therefore selected that position to gain more honour. The officers and gentlemen in the battle were Lieutenant-Colonel Purdon, commanding the whole; Captains Kingston and Rogers; and Lieutenant Calder of the Royal African corps; Dr. Young of the staff; Mr. Henry Richter, merchant, of Danish Accra, with his own men, amounting to about one hundred and twenty; Mr. J. W. Hanson, merchant, of British Accra, with his men, in number nearly the same; Mr. John Jackson, merchant, of Cape Coast, with Mr. Bannerman's men, about the same number, Mr. Bannerman being absent in England in bad health; and Mr. Hutchinson, merchant, of Annamaboe, with the Cape Coast artificers, volunteers; part of the townspeople; and Bynie, the native chief, whose people, with the others, amounted to one hundred and fifty men. These formed the centre, and were drawn up in line with the Royal African corps, as a reserve on the position previously taken by Captain Kingston.

The attack commenced from right to left, at about half past nine o'clock. Several of the natives came insulting and abusing the centre as cowards; which being represented to the commanding officer, he directed them to advance about four hundred yards, when a heavy and effective fire took place. They went steadily forward amid the work of death, the enemy slowly and sulkily giving way. No prisoners were taken by the natives, but as they fell they were put to death: happy were they whose sufferings were short; in vain the gentlemen implored them to hold their hand, or at least to kill them outright; some were ripped up and cut across the belly, when plunging their hands in, they took out the heart, pouring the blood on the ground as a libation to the good fortune of the cause: others, when they saw their own friends weltering in their blood, would give them a blow on the breast or head, to put an end to their misery.

In many instances they dragged each other from the opposite ranks and wrestled and cut one another in pieces; and fortunate was he whose knife first found out the vital part in his foe during the deadly grapple, though perhaps in his turn to be laid low by the same means. So hard were the enemy pressed at this moment, that a captain of consequence blew himself up, nearly involving some of the Europeans in destruction.

The number of the various articles taken from the enemy was very great, but as none were allowed to leave the field, and as they had no spare hands, like the people of the native chiefs, they were thrown aside, when a cry arose that the Ashantees were getting between the centre and the left, which was the fact, as one party from the Dutch town, who supported the right of the Cape Coast people, had given way, and the enemy had rushed into their place. Besides this, the whole of the Danish natives, with their *caboceers* at their head, had fled early in the action, and the swallow-tailed banners of Denmark were seen safely flying in the rear. The centre were now obliged to fall back and relinquish every advantage, sustaining a galling fire in flank, and closely pressed with the mass of the enemy, who evidently were making a bold push to seize or bring down the whites.

Captain Rogers, who was advancing with a small piece of artillery, would have been taken, had he not very promptly distinguished them as the enemy. This was the crisis of the battle; Colonel Purdon advanced with the reserve, and the rockets, a few of which thrown among the Ashantees occasioned the most dreadful havoc and confusion: the hissing sound when thrown, the train of fire, the explosion and frightful wounds they inflicted, caused them to suppose that they were thunder and lightning, called *snowman* in Fantee, by which name they are now known among the natives.

Another party of Ashantees having attacked the left of King Cheboe of Dinkera, the Winnebahs fled at the first fire, nor halted till they reached Accra, but a few rounds of grape shot, thrown over the heads of our people, restored the battle there also, Cheboe being already in advance with part of his people driving back his opponents. On the right, the battle was not for a moment doubtful; the king of Akimboo drove all before him, and penetrating to the King of Ashantee's camp, took them in flank; his path was marked by the column of smoke that rose in front, the short grass being dry, from our forces having bivouacked at the roots of the trees for two nights, together with extreme heat, caused it to take fire; the explosions of some Ashantee captains, who at intervals blew themselves up in despair, which was known by the smoke that arose over the trees; the shouts and groans of the combatants, with the burning grass, and the battle raging all around, formed no bad idea of the infernal regions.

Fancy may indeed imagine, but it cannot describe such a scene of havoc and destruction, more resembling the wild fiction of an oriental tale, than one of absolute reality. The Danish natives who had fled at nearly the first onset, now perceiving the enemy to be repulsed by the rockets and grape shot, advanced, and taking possession of the plunder, which was immense, deliberately walked off the field; they sent to request more ammunition, saying they had only received twenty rounds each from their own government; and when upbraided with their bad conduct, they said it was against their fetish to fire on a Monday. About one o'clock, the heads of the Ashantee chiefs began to be brought in.

Several of the blood royal and principal captains were known by the residents; when the deaths of any of them were reported to the king, he offered up human sacrifices to their manes in the heat of the battle. Among the sad trophies of the day, was supposed to be the head of Sir Charles MacCarthy, which was sent to England by Lieutenant-Colonel Purdon; it was taken by the Aquapim chief. The king carried it along with him as a powerful charm, and on the morning of the battle, he poured rum upon it, and invoked it to cause all the heads of the whites on the field to lie beside it. The skull was enveloped in paper covered with Arabic characters, and a silk handkerchief, over all was a tiger skin, the emblem of royalty.

The whole of the Ashantee camp was taken, together with their baggage and gold; the amount of the latter was said to be very considerable, but the whites never could ascertain what the natives obtained. Towards the end of the day, a great many slaves or prisoners were taken by the natives, who subsequently sold them to slave vessels to leeward of Accra, being satiated with the multitudes they had killed, in the early part of the fight, and until it was dark, parties were coming in with plunder from every quarter.

The troops lay on their arms all night, as it was not known but that the king, with his surviving friends, might make an attack upon us in despair, having been seen in front, wandering over the scene of his blighted ambition. Through the night, at intervals, some of our native allied chiefs struck their drums to some recitations, which were repeated along the line, and as they died away, had a most pleasing effect, but were generally succeeded by deep wailings and lamentations from the glades, in front of our position, apparently from some unhappy Ashantee women looking for their friends among the fallen.

The loss of chiefs on our part was but small; Mr. Richter was wounded in the thigh early in the action, and obliged to leave the field, but his men did not follow the flying portion of their countrymen. Narboah, the captain-general of the Akimboos, the chief captain of the queen of Akim, and Quashie Amonquah, chief of Esseecoomah, were the only persons of rank that we lost. The latter was regretted by everyone, as several of the natives were always accusing him of treachery, and he was determined to shew in the day of battle his sincerity, he therefore made a bold attempt to seize the king's person, and to take him dead or alive, and even had his hand on the royal basket to pull him down, when he was shot in the neck and secured.

The king upbraided him for his treachery, and ordered him to follow, which he refused; order was then given to decapitate him; a party of Cheboos attacked the king, but Amonquah was already killed, and his head, if they have preserved it, is the only trophy which they can exhibit. His brother Abaggy was wounded in the thigh, or, as he says, "he would have made the king pay dear for his brother's head," which none doubted.

The number of our forces, from the best information, amounted to eleven thousand; three hundred and eighty with muskets; that of the enemy was estimated at ten thousand, and much of the fighting was with the knife. We calculated our loss at about eight hundred killed and one thousand slightly wounded. The enemy it is supposed must have lost full five thousand men: a great many of their chief men were killed, whose names were familiar to African readers: among them were Bundahin, the king's uncle; Yeou Corowco, the captain who carried the gold stool; Karcum, the chief linguist; Adoo Bradie, nephew to the king, long resident at Cape Coast; Adoo Quamina, mentioned in Mr. Dupuis' residence in Ashantee; Fosoo Crah, well known along the coast, where he used to collect tribute; Gamadooah, the same; Yaw Sackery, who carried on a long war with the Akimfoos; Damachies, Apookoo's son, the native who captured Sir Charles MacCarthy at Assamacow and who took all the ammunition; Owoosoe Yaw Coomah, Oroosoe Aquahteah, Oroosoe Domra. Attah Quam. Adjuampon Entyquah, the Assim traitor, shot himself, Acrahsoh Coffee, Adaboy, Quaw Cultaqua, Samponday, and four others; twenty-four chiefs in all. Osai Accato, the king, was wounded; Opokoo, the chief instigator of the war, was severely scorched with powder and died in consequence.

Among the prisoners were, Oroosoe Doome, the last Ashantee resident at Cape Coast in 1818; Oroosoe Ansan, the boy king of Enclensah, beyond Ashantee. The King of Ashantee's Crabah, a female dedicated to the *sooman, fetish*, one of his wives, and a female child, one of his *occras*, or page, a male dedicated to the *sooman* Enteyquah's wife, Yaw Sackery's wife, Yawmadoo's child, Otill, king's linguist, one of Boetine king of Bewobin's *accras*.

It may be readily supposed that the chiefs would have gone in pursuit of the fugitive king after such a decisive day, but on the contrary, all of them, with their people, returned to Accra, groaning under their immense booty. If the Ashantees had delayed the battle a few weeks, the coalition would have fallen to pieces, for the natives, abandoned to themselves, would not have stood half an hour before the enemy. To shew what contrivances and resources this singular people have, it may be mentioned that in the "wallets" of some who fell, were found the *pangolin*, (see note following), or ant eater, scorched for food, while instead of shot among other things were found *cowrie* shells loaded with lead. The Danish *caboceer* used every artifice to bring on a battle before the other chiefs could arrive, and kept moving to the east to facilitate this project, while the others followed to avoid quarrels.

******

Note:—The *pangolin*, which is a native of the torrid climates of Africa, is incapable of being carnivorous, since it has no teeth, but lives entirely on insects which nature has fitted in a very extraordinary manner. As it has a long nose, so it may naturally be supposed to have a long tongue, but to increase its length still more, it is doubled in the mouth, so that when extended, it is shot out above a quarter of a yard. When the *pangolin*, therefore, approaches an ant-hill, it lies down near it, concealing as much as possible the place of its retreat, and stretching its long tongue among the ants, keeps it for some time immovable. These little animals, allured by its appearance, and the unctuous substance, gather upon it in great numbers, and when the *pangolin* supposes a sufficiency, it quickly withdraws the tongue, and swallows them at once. It is, of all other animals, the best protected from external injury by nature. It is about three feet long; or taking in the tail, from six to eight.

Like the lizard, it has a small head, a very long nose, a short thick neck, a long body, legs very short, and tail extremely long, thick at insertion, and terminating in a point. It has no teeth, but is armed with five toes on each foot, with white long claws. But what it is chiefly distinguished by, is its scaly covering, which, in some measure, hides all the proportions of its body. These scales defend the animal on all parts, except the under part of the head and neck, under the shoulders, the breast, the belly, and the inner sides of the legs; all which parts are covered with a smooth, soft skin, without hair. The scales of this extraordinary creature are of different sizes and different forms, and stuck on the body like the leaves of an artichoke, the largest are found near the tail, these are above three inches broad, and about two inches long; they are extremely hard, and resemble horn.

Thus armed, this animal fears nothing from the efforts of all other creatures, except man. The instant it perceives the approach of an enemy, it rolls itself up like the hedgehog, and presents no part but the cutting edges of its scales to the assailants. Its shells are so large, so thick, and so pointed, that they repel every animal of prey. The most cruel quadruped of the forest make vain attempts to force it, but to no purpose, the *pangolin* remains safe within, while its invader almost always feels the rewards of its rashness.—*Lynnaeus, Syst. Nat. tom.* 1. p. 36.

✶✶✶✶✶✶

It was singular to see some of the natives under the Dutch flag fighting by our side, while, had we been at Elmina, they probably would have been found in the opposing ranks, as some of them were at Affettue. The Queen of Akim, who evinced much activity in the war, is about five feet three inches in height, with an infantine look; her voice is soft, evidently modulated to interest her audience, but cracked as a singer would express it, from constant use. She is an excellent beggar for munitions of war and distilled waters: just before the attack she went along the line with a massive necklace of leaden bullets, and in her hand a gold enamelled cutlass, and she was afterwards in the hottest part of the action. To some of the gentlemen who called on her the day before, she said among other things, "Osai has driven me from my country because he thought me weak, but though I am a woman, I have the heart of a man."

Thus terminated the most important battle ever fought on this coast, and which will in all probability deter these people from disturbing the country again, at least for a long time in a hostile manner.

CHAPTER 8

Terms of Peace Proposed

Sir Neil Campbell disembarked at Cape Coast on the 21st; and Lieutenant-Colonel Purdon having obtained leave to return to England, the governor was pleased to appoint Captain Ricketts to the military and civil command of the Gold Coast, in his stead. Immediately after the governor landed, he received the king, the *caboceers*, and the head men of Cape Coast, and congratulated them upon the recent victory obtained by the British troops commanded by Lieutenant-Colonel Purdon, the militia of Cape Coast, their countrymen, commanded by Mr. Hutchinson, and the native kings and chiefs, allies of the King of England; and he added, that this victory would probably insure an advantageous and permanent peace, from which trade would be carried on from the coast to the interior without any interruption. Nothing further was said, and all separated as soon as His Excellency left the hall of the castle.

On the 26th of September, the following chiefs assembled in the hall at Cape Coast Castle, by desire of His Excellency, messengers having been dispatched for them; *viz*. Cudjoe Cheboo, King of Dinkera; Awoosooco, King of Tueful; Ahmonee, and Baffoe, chiefs of Annamaboe; Adookoo, King of Fantee; kings and headmen of Cape Coast. He thanked them in the name of the king of England for their bravery in the battle; and said, as the king of the Ashantees was now so humbled, it was the best time to let him know, that if he would send messengers to him for peace, it might be granted, on giving security for his peaceable conduct in future towards the king of England and each of them. To this proposal they objected, stating that they knew the King of Ashantee too well to suppose that he would not construe such a message into submission on our part.

His Excellency then told them that peace would not be granted, unless sufficient security was given to each of them, to remain in his own country, without danger; that he would not make peace for the King of England separately, but for all; that the object of going to war was to obtain peace; that if we had lost a battle, this proposal might be ascribed to fear, but not after such a victory. They then asked for a delay of twelvemonths, stating that the Ashantees would in that time solicit peace; but the governor not acceding to their request, they said that they would not make any promise unless all the allies were consulted; the governor observed that the distance of the others, *viz.* the Queen of Akim, the King of Aquamboe, and the chief of Aquapim, rendered it impossible to confer with them at the same time, but messengers had been sent to Captain Kingston to assemble them at Accra, as the proposed delay would be contrary to the orders of the king of England.

After saying much more to the same effect, he at last told them that his orders to make peace were peremptory, and that he must obey them, without any stipulation in their favour, if they would not consent to send to the King of Ashantee. His Excellency then gave them some presents for their bravery; informing them at the same time that his determination to make peace was not to be changed.

The kings and chiefs still remaining in Cape Coast, the governor resolved to send a few presents by the most direct road to Coomassie. The King of Cape Coast was directed to select three intelligent men, one of whom could write, to proceed openly with a paper containing what he wished to say to the King of Ashantee. The Kings of Dinkera, Tueful, Wassaw, Fantee, and the chiefs of the Assin country, were also directed to send a few persons as an escort, but which they refused. It was reported that the kings of Dinkera and Tueful had said, that if the mission met with any harm, it would be their own fault in quitting Cape Coast; by this it was supposed that they wished to intimidate them from undertaking it.

His Excellency upon hearing of this, sent for the King of Dinkera, but he did not attend; not from any disrespect to the governor as it afterwards appeared, but from fear that he might be detained a prisoner in the castle, and be delivered up to the Ashantees in order to obtain peace. The governor then sent for a few of their people, and directed them to inform the kings of Dinkera and Tueful, that in one hour they and every one of their followers should leave the town, for their disrespect to him on this occasion; the projected mission to the Ashantees was in consequence abandoned. On the 10th of October the governor proceeded to Accra, but the chiefs who were expected did not assemble, being under Danish influence.

Sir Neil Campbell returned to Cape Coast on the 19th. On the day of his departure from Accra, Cudjoe Cheboo, the King of Dinkera, sent two messengers to request his forgiveness; they were received by the King of Cape Coast, but he did not, as was customary, acquaint the commandant of their arrival, but informed them of the governor's departure, and said that on his return he would send to acquaint him of it, which he did accordingly, but not as from the governor. His Excellency sailed on the 15th of November for Sierra Leone. On the 15th of January messengers arrived at Cape Coast from the Assins to Caboceer Bynie, acquainting him that some people from Adansay, a place adjoining the Ashantee country, and a day's journey from Coomassie, where the Assins had resided since they deserted from the Ashantees, requesting of him to ask the commandant to find some person to be present with those expected from the different allied chiefs, for the purpose of hearing what they had to propose.

The commandant told the Assin messengers to inform their chiefs that he was obliged to them for their proposed interview, but that he could not, as commandant of the British forces, condescend to send any persons to meet messengers from the chiefs alluded to, and that Cape Coast was the proper place for the people from Adansay to deliver their proposals; but that he had not any objection to the king and *caboceers* of Cape Coast sending two or three men to be present, when the people from Adansay might state their object. Two men from the chiefs were accordingly sent, and after staying in that country a considerable time, they returned to Cape Coast, and said that the people from Adansay did not wish to come to Cape Coast, as it might be supposed that they had something of importance to communicate, whereas they were only desired by their chiefs to discover where the Assins were, and then to return immediately. About three weeks after this the chiefs of the Assins sent for the two Cape Coast messengers, stating that the Adansay people wished to return home, and that the Assin chiefs were desirous they should be present for the purpose of hearing what message would be sent to Coomassie.

The messengers were accordingly sent up, having first been instructed by the commandant and the native chiefs what to say on behalf of them, and the Cape Coast people, in case any message likely to prolong the war was sent to the Ashantees.

After the Cape Coast messengers had remained at Yancoomassie for three weeks, or more, and none of those expected from the different tribes appearing, the chiefs of Assin sent one of them down to say that it appeared that none of the chiefs had any intention of sending to hear what might be said to the Adansays on their returning home. The *commandant*, immediately on hearing this, dispatched two trusty soldiers with instructions to proceed to Yancoomassie, and to acquaint the Assin chiefs that he wished to send a message to the King of Ashantee, which they were to deliver to the people from Adansay, in their (the chiefs of Assins, presence. The message was as follows:—

That the commandant had received orders to make peace with the Ashantees for the English, and for such of the native tribes as were desirous of being included in this pacific proposal; and that if the Ashantees were inclined to peace, he should be happy to see any of them at Cape Coast for that purpose; that should they be afraid of obstruction in their way down, he would, on being acquainted therewith through the Assins, take measures to secure their safety both in coming and in returning.

The soldiers accordingly accompanied the Adansay people a considerable distance on their way home from Yancoomassie. The Assins sent four men with them to Adansay, with directions to return in thirty days from the 14th of May.

A few days before the time appointed for their return, a sergeant with some soldiers was dispatched, accompanied by messengers from the chiefs, to wait their arrival at Yancoomassie, with orders to escort any messengers from Ashantee direct to Cape Coast; but it was long after the time fixed before the Assin messengers returned, in company with nine men from Adansay, bringing a message from the chief of that place to Cape Coast, importing that the chief of Adansay was the person who settled all differences between the Ashantees and those at war with them; that he wished the commandant of Cape Coast, and all the allied chiefs, to send messengers to him, then he could see the King of Ashantee respecting peace. The commandant knowing that none of the native allied chiefs would consent to send, or allow persons from him to pass to Coomassie, desired the messengers to wait a few days, and he would give them an answer: accordingly on the 14th of May he made the following reply:

> Tell the King of Adansay I am much obliged to him for his goodness; that the king of England wants no war with the natives of Africa; justice is all that is required; there is no war in

any other country but this; all is peace and happiness. That if the King of Ashantee is willing to make peace, and if he will send to Adansay proper persons for that purpose, I will, on being acquainted therewith through the Assins, send up a guard to meet them halfway: that the Ashantees need not be afraid of sending to Cape Coast, as I and the Cape Coast people will take care that none of them shall be molested, either in coming or returning; and when peace shall be made, all quarrels will be forgotten.

On the 25th of July, 1827, a follower of Quashie Amonquah, a chief who fought with the Ashantees against us at Cape Coast, on the 11th of July, and who afterwards joined us, and fought against the Ashantees in the Battle of Dodoowah, and was there killed, was this day brought a prisoner to Cape Coast, charged by the allies with having gone secretly to Adansay, and pretended that he had been sent by the *commandant* of Cape Coast with a message to the King of Ashantee. The following are the real particulars: this man being in debt, and having obtained a roll of Portuguese tobacco, was desirous of making the most of it, and conceiving that he would be able to dispose of it to greater advantage at Coomassie than elsewhere, in consequence of the suspension of all trade by the war with that place, he accordingly proceeded thither, and on arriving at Adansay, a day's journey from Coomassie, he was asked who had sent him, to which he replied, that the *commandant* of Cape Coast, and Mr. Hutchinson, of Annamaboe, had desired him to inform the King of Ashantee, that white men did not fight always, and would make peace if the King of Ashantee wished it.

The chief of Adansay replied, that he would not believe he was sent by the persons whom he had named, or he would not have been alone; to which he replied, that if they did not believe him, they might cut off his head, then they would see what a palaver they would get with the white men. On his being asked what had induced him to make use of the *commandant's* and Mr. Hutchison's names, he answered, that he did so in hopes this might have influence in preserving his life. The tobacco was taken from him by the Adansays, and for it he received payment. What he had said was reported to the King of Ashantee, who sent him four *ackies* and half in gold for subsistence. The Assin messengers who accompanied the first mission from Adansay back to that place, saw this man there, and on their return, reporting the circumstance to their chiefs, they sent to enquire of the commandant whether this man's information was correct and true, which being answered in the negative, they told the Adansays if the Ashantees were sincere in wishing for peace, it would be shewn by this man being sent to them, which was immediately complied with.

The Assin chiefs, in asking for the man, remarked to the Adansays, that if persons of this description were permitted to pass backwards and forwards before peace was concluded, they might carry such stories as would put a stop to the proceedings necessary to effect that object. The messenger who returned on the night of the 21st from Yancoomassie, was on the 26th of July sent back, conveying orders that the soldiers should take it in turns to proceed to Weakering, a village on the banks of the Pra, in order to take care that the expected Ashantee mission met with no interruption in its way down to the coast. The *commandant* was apprehensive that some obstacles might be thrown in the way, by some of the native chiefs, who had been for some time assembled in the Braffoe country for the purpose of extorting money from the Ashantees.

Information therefore being given on the 2nd of August, that the Ashantee mission was expected to arrive at Yancoomassie on the next day; in order to keep his promise to the Ashantees, and to guard against their being molested by the natives in their way to Cape Coast, he immediately dispatched a respectable man, a sergeant in the militia, and a messenger from the natives of the town, with directions to acquaint the native chiefs that it was his positive orders that these people should not be detained, but allowed to proceed without molestation to Cape Coast, and that they were to be very active in ascertaining what was going forward, taking care to report to the *commandant* every circumstance of importance.

One of the men returned from Yancoomassie on the 6th of August, and stated that the chief of Adansay had informed the Assin chiefs, that in consequence of the man who went to that place and made use of the *commandant's* name, having been demanded by the allied chiefs, and the King of Ashantee understanding that the man was a prisoner, he was afraid to send messengers to Cape Coast, unless the chiefs of Adansay would take fetish that they would not incur any danger; in consequence of which the soldier was desired to return to Yancoomassie, accompanied by the man alluded to, whom the *commandant* had demanded of the allies and kept in the castle to prevent his experiencing any harm, with directions for the soldiers and messengers to proceed to Adansay without delay, taking the man with them, and to acquaint the chief of that place that they were sent to him in consequence of what he had told the Assins; and that the man, who being present, could speak for himself, was found fault with only for having in an unauthorised manner made use of the *commandant's* name; that they were desired to wait at Adansay until the King of Ashantee sent down persons to make peace should he be so inclined.

The *commandant* sent also by a man who could read and write, a paper containing as follows:—

> The Governor of Cape Coast understanding through the Assins, that the King of Ashantee did not like to send persons to Cape Coast to make peace, being doubtful whether they would be safe from the circumstance of the man who went to Adansay, and made use of his name, having been demanded by some of the allied chiefs and kept a prisoner; the governor therefore sends that man and some soldiers to tell the King of Ashantee, that the path is opened for any of his people to come to Cape Coast for the purpose of making peace, and should the king wish it, they are to remain at Adansay, until his messengers are ready to escort them down.
> The Governor of Cape Coast sends a book of God, (an Arabic bible, in hopes some of the Moors who frequent Coomassie may be able to read it,) to the King of Ashantee, that he may believe what the governor says is true, and that no harm will happen to any of his people whom he may send to Cape Coast.

The commandant further gave orders, that if no objection was made on the part of the chief of Adansay, the man alluded to by the King of Ashantee should be sent to Coomassie with the bible abovementioned. The *commandant*, in order to shew the Ashantees that he was not displeased with the man, gave him some presents, and entrusted him with a silver medal as a token that he came from him.

A general report prevailed on the 8th of August that the Ashantee messengers had arrived at Dansamansue, on this side of the Pra, about the 1st of this month, and that they were concealed until it might suit the purpose of the King of Dinkera to let them pass to Cape Coast. The *commandant* sent to acquaint their chiefs of his having heard the above report, and if true to desire that the Ashantee messengers should immediately be allowed to proceed to Cape Coast, otherwise he would consider them as his enemies. The Cape Coast chiefs at this news were much incensed against them.

The messengers returned on the 8th, and stated that Adookoo, King of Fantee; Annimelli, King of Wassaw; Cudjoe Cheboo, King of Dinkera; Awoosooko, chief of Tueful; Braffoe and Ahmonee, *caboceer* of Annamaboe; with several other petty chiefs, the whole of whom were assembled in the Braffoe country, sent their respects to their master, meaning the *commandant*, and informed him that they had not assembled on account of the mission expected from the Ashantees, but to arrange matters regarding themselves; that no messengers had to their knowledge, crossed the Pra; but should any arrive, they would be sent to Cape Coast.

The mission which was sent to Adansay was prevented proceeding further than Yancoomassie by the Assins, who said that they could not allow even a white man to pass to Adansay; that they had commenced the negotiation for peace, and wished to reap themselves the benefit that might arise from it.

On the 1st of September, two messengers arrived from the Assins, and stated that messengers had arrived from the King of Ashantee and were actually within a days march of Yancoomassie. The *commandant* having been several times deceived by similar messages from that tribe, and although he was convinced that the present information was correct, having received the same account from other quarters, yet he told the Assins he would not believe them, unless they brought one of the Ashantees to him. This day the same Assin messengers returned to Cape Coast, bringing with them two men, attached to the Ashantee mission, which had now arrived at Yancoomassie. All the merchants were in consequence assembled in the government hall, at the castle, when the following message from the Ashantees was delivered in their presence to the commandant.

> That the King of Ashantee found it was no use in fighting against white men, and wished to make peace and to be in future subservient to the white men; that His Majesty had sent down proper persons to make peace; who, with followers amounting to one hundred and forty, were at Yancoomassie.

The *commandant*, in reply told them, that he was very glad to see them, as they had come to do what was good for the country, and that therefore they were welcome to Cape Coast. He sent some rum to them, that they might drink the King of England's health.

On the 11th of October, the lieutenant-governor, Lieutenant-Colonel Lumley arrived from Sierra Leone, in His Majesty's ship *Eden*, Captain W. F. Owen. The escort sent to meet the messengers from the King of Ashantee returned on the 18th of October, with a part of them, leaving the especial messenger from the King of Ashantee at Yancoomassie, the Assins being afraid to send him down until the whole of the allied chiefs agreed to it, the natives having entertained an idea that the white men wished to make peace with the Ashantees; without them, their distrust was excited, and this caused the detention of the Ashantee messengers who it was reported had been a long time on the way from Coomassie to Cape Coast.

Cabooceer Bynie having volunteered to go to Yancoomassie, returned with the messengers on the 23rd, accompanied by the chiefs of Fantee and Assin. The Ashantee messengers were presented to the lieutenant-governor who had assembled all the officers and merchants to receive them: great form was observed by the messengers, one of them, a relation of the king, had on a cap made of monkey-skin; it had a tail which hung down on the back of his neck; on the front of the cap, was a gold plate, about five inches long and two inches broad, upon which scales were neatly represented.

On this man being desired to deliver his message, he took off his cap, and gave it to the chief of Assin, who handed it to one of the Fantee chiefs, and he to another, and lastly to the king of Cape Coast, who delivered it to the lieutenant-governor. The messenger then said that the King of Ashantee was very sorry for what he had done, and hoped that the English would pardon him; that he found there was no use in his fighting against white men, and therefore wished to be under their control, and as a token of his submission, he now laid his cap at the King of England's feet.

On the 12th of December, several chiefs, *viz.* the Kings of Wassaw, Dinkera, Assin, Fantee, Tueful, Annamaboe, Cape Coast, and many others of minor note, being assembled according to notice sent to them, the following terms were agreed to, as being those on which peace would be granted to the Ashantees, *viz.*,—that they should lodge four thousand ounces of gold in the Castle of Cape Coast, to be appropriated in purchasing ammunition and arms for the use of the British allies, in case the Ashantees should again commence hostilities; and that two of the royal family of Ashantee, whose names were mentioned, should be sent to Cape Coast as hostages.

The King of Accombo, the Queen of Akim, the chiefs of Aquapim and the Accras were not present at the meeting, but messengers from each of them arrived a few days after, and the terms on which peace had been offered being explained to them, they signified their approval on the parts of their respective chiefs.

Several attempts were made to ascertain from the Ashantee messengers some particulars connected with the several actions, but no satisfactory reply could be obtained. It appeared that they acted as spies on each other, for they would not give an answer to any question without first consulting among themselves. The only information we obtained was, that there were at Coomassie a white man taken at Affettue, and a *mulatto* man of Cape Coast, taken at Assamacow. The Ashantee messengers, after remaining at Cape Coast a few days longer, departed for Coomassie, accompanied by a respectable native named John Carr, and a lad of colour, named John Buckman, who was also a native and educated at Cape Coast, selected for that purpose; and messengers from most of the native allies.

The party arrived at Coomassie on the 4th of February, as will appear by the following extract of a letter written by the lad of colour, copied *verbatim*:—

> Now for the news? we arrived here on the fourth instant in the morning about seven; the king and his people assembled and saluted us in public manner, and also many strange things I saw on that day: about two hundred men carrying golden swords, and also skulls moulted of gold, everything about of him gold. When we went before him, he sat on his higher throne, and when he saw us, he made his hand a motion to pass, when he did not say with his mouth, after he sat he also came with his chiefs and saluted us; all the great umbrellas appeared on that day was two hundred and thirty. Interview on the next morning he sent us presents of pigs, and sheep, plantains, yams, and some other things, also four ounces and eight *ackies* of gold between me and Mr. Carr. Indeed he has treated us very well for to do this.
>
> Now as I am writing this, his sister has send us five *ackies* of gold and the above like. Since we arrived, the inhabitants has not fail of playing of rejoice for peace. On the Sunday last, the tenth, they killed a man; very large European house they have erected here, if you know Amorah of Accra I would say that the king's form like him, also his manners; he is very good king, because

he has, since we arrived, behaved very well to us; every day he sends us couple of pots of palm wine, sometimes four, and also his people they speak very well to make peace, only they had some doubt on the part of the Assins, and Cudjoe Cheboo; this is all the news I could send you at present. We arrived on the fourth.

Shortly after this the white man alluded to as being prisoner at Coomassie, and who proved to be private Patrick Riley, of the Royal African Corps, taken prisoner on the 25th of April, 1824, with the man of colour, John Duncan, a private in the militia, taken in the battle near Assamacow, on the 24th of January, 1824, were sent to Cape Coast by the King of Ashantee, accompanied by messengers from him, who stated that the king, in order to shew the Europeans his sincerity in wishing for peace, had immediately, on being made acquainted with the governor's wish to have these two persons returned, sent them down, and that in return the king requested that some of his family might be sent, particularly his head wife, who had been taken prisoner at Doodowah, and to allow one of his chief Achampong, and some of his subjects, who were prevented by the allies from returning to Coomassie, by keeping such a strict watch over Elmina; that he would, on these terms being complied with, endeavour to collect the sum demanded of him as security for his good behaviour and send it down.

But his request could not be complied with, as the king's wife had been taken prisoner by some native chief under Danish influence, and as the Danes were dissatisfied as regarded their own security with the proposed arrangement they signified their intention of making peace for themselves, and which the possession of this female would probably induce the king to grant more readily, and the whole of the native allies had signified their determination not to allow any of the Ashantees at Elmina to return to their country until the King of Ashantee had given proper security for his peaceful behaviour.

The European soldier and the man of colour stated that the king had behaved well to them during the whole period they were prisoners at Coomassie. Riley said, he had enjoyed better health while there (a period of four years) than when at Cape Coast; but he appeared confused in his ideas, and having been kept at a small village a short distance from Coomassie, where he was only allowed to walk about, he could give but an indifferent account of the country. He related the following statement of his capture. On information reaching Affettue that the Ashantees who had defeated the allies on the 25th of April, were in quick advance on that place, the troops in consequence commenced their retreat to Cape Coast; he however, with two other European soldiers of the Royal African Corps, remained behind, and got possession of some ration rum that had arrived for the troops: on some of the enemy coming to the premises where they were, one of them fixed his bayonet and charged them; and they immediately decapitated him.

Riley and the other remaining quiet, their lives were spared , they were, however, stripped of their cloathing and disarmed, and Ashantee cloaths were given to them to wrap round their bodies. They were shortly after sent to Coomassie, where his companion died in about twelve months. Riley was a few months after his return to Cape Coast, sent to England.

His Majesty's brig of war, *Clinker*, having arrived to convey Lieutenant-Colonel Lumley to Sierra Leone, he embarked, leaving Captain Kingston in command at Cape Coast. The service requiring that Major Ricketts should go to Sierra Leone, he had sailed on the 9th of January.

The merchants being desirous that this officer should continue in command of the Gold Coast, signified their wish to Lieutenant-Colonel Lumley shortly after his arrival at Cape Coast, in a letter in which they had occasion to address him on the 19th of October, in the following words:—

> We indulge the hope that Captain Ricketts will be continued in command; his judicious and conciliatory measures having established such confidence in the minds of the natives as to induce them to place much reliance on the equity of his proceedings, and having succeeded in opening a communication with the Ashantees, part of an embassy from whom now are in this town and the remainder only twenty-four miles inland.

The town had been greatly improved by Major Ricketts, he caused all the houses to be moved which overlooked the ramparts of the castle, and others which interfered with the range of guns, and formed some good streets in the town. Lieutenant-Colonel Lumley, on Major Ricketts leaving the Gold Coast, issued a general order to the following effect.

Cape Coast Castle, January 5th, 1828.
The Lieutenant-Colonel commanding has much pleasure in recording how much he is obliged to Captain Ricketts for his conduct in opening a communication with the Ashantee nation, from which the best results may be expected; namely, the procuring a permanent peace with that power and the neighbouring tribes. The lieutenant-colonel also feels indebted to Captain Ricketts for the manner in which the castle and forts have been put into their present good repair, and respectable state of defence, and which object has been obtained with great economy of the public money.

At the latter end of April, the following letter was received at Cape Coast by Captain Kingston from the King of Ashantee, brought by the lad of colour, Buckman, at his majesty's desire.

Saturday Morning, Coomassie Castle,
12th April, 1828.

Sir,

I beg to acknowledge your letter of the 9th of last month, and on which I took it into consideration of granting your request; but as I received some information that Fantees are already marched for Elmina, to put me in great doubt with all my people, I thought when the peace was concluded would for all my subjects. Therefore I send your messenger, Mr. John Buckman, with my messenger, so that you will see into and settle them for peace. If such made by you, will get some of the Ashantees that are at Elmina to come with Mr. John Buckman on his return. I beg to inform you that the amount of the security of four thousand ounces of gold, that was too much; but however as my ancestors has lodged four hundred ounces, for the security of friendship, I beg to do the same; and as soon as Mr. Buckman will return, I shall speedily return them with such amount. I beg to inform the reason Mr. Carr so stopped. If I do send him without the demand, would seem if not liking to make peace, and not regarding you; therefore I beg you will excuse me.

  I have the honour to be. Sir,
    your humble servant,

Osai Coutoe,
+ his mark.

Witnesses, John Carr, John Buckman.

Colonel Lumley having left instructions with Captain Kingston not to make any alterations in the terms offered to the Ashantees for peace, he made the following reply:

Cape Coast Castle, May 1, 1828.

Sir,

I have the honour to acknowledge the receipt of your letter dated 12th of April, 1828, relative to the pending negotiations for peace: in reply, I have to inform you that no other terms can be acceded to than those originally proposed, *viz.* four thousand ounces of gold to be lodged in this castle, as well as two principal persons to be sent as hostages for the future tranquillity of the coast. That as soon as the above terms are complied with, and not before, Achampong and his companions at Elmina will be allowed to return to Coomassie.

If the terms proposed are not acceded to by your majesty within twenty days after the arrival of John Buckman and the messengers at Coomassie, you will order John Buckman and the other persons from the Cape Coast to return; or if you wish Carr to remain, that some Ashantee chief be sent to reside at Cape Coast. The dispute between the Fantees and Elminas cannot be allowed to interfere with the more important question between the British and Ashantees. None of the Cape Coast people have joined in the war against Elmina. That on peace being concluded, every exertion will be made in conjunction with the governor of Elmina, to arrange the dispute between the Fantees and Elminas. I send to your majesty three Ashantee prisoners, who were captured during the war.

I have the honour to remain, with sincerity,
your most humble servant,

J. Hingston
Captain and Commandant.

To His Majesty, Osai Cootoe, King of Ashantee.

CHAPTER 9

Conclusion of a Final Peace

The native tribes, who joined in the war against the Ashantees, were highly incensed against the natives of Elmina for not taking part with them in it, and instead of remaining neutral, as they had signified their determination, assisted the Ashantees by supplying them with munitions of war, and conveyed to them information of our movements, which they were enabled to do from the uninterrupted intercourse they had with Cape Coast. Although the governor of Elmina used every means in his power to prevent gunpowder being supplied by the natives of that place to the Ashantees, yet the following statement will shew how they acted in this respect.

An American vessel arriving there with gunpowder on board, when the Ashantees were in the immediate vicinity of Cape Coast, the governor would not allow any to be landed, but it was reported to him a few days after the vessel had anchored, that a quantity had been sold to some of the natives of Elmina and taken away at night by them in canoes. As none of it could be found in the town, it was supposed that it had been sent to the Ashantees. The Fantees had long borne their hatred to the Elminas, on account, as they stated, that when the Ashantee Army invaded Fantee, and attacked Annamaboe Fort in 1807, many of the women, children, and infirm men had sought refuge at Elmina, and carried with them a good deal of property; that the Elminas delivered many of them up to the Ashantees, who sold them for slaves, and appropriated their valuables to their own use.

With these feelings the natives who had fought against the Ashantees, with the exception of those at, and in the neighbourhood of the Accras, engaged to attack Elmina; and in pursuance of this determination, strengthened by the knowledge that the Ashantees were unable, from the recent defeats, to send an army to the relief of the Elminas, commenced encamping in the vicinity of that place, soon after the last meeting of the native chiefs of Cape Coast. They had then stated their grievances to Lieutenant-Colonel Lumley, and said they would be satisfied if the Elminas paid the Fantees a certain sum of money, for the losses already enumerated, which they declared they had sustained. Colonel Lumley wrote to the governor of Elmina on the subject, who replied that the Elminas denied the accusation, and refused to pay any thing. The intention of these people at first was, as they said, to endeavour to bring the Elminas to their terms by cutting off all supplies by land at least, for they were unable to accomplish that object by water, and by destroying the provisions in the neighbourhood of that place.

This they succeeded in accomplishing in a great measure, which induced the Elminas to cultivate the land within the range of the guns of Fort St. Jago, which is built on a hill a little distance from the castle, and some outworks, which were thought necessary, from these circumstances, to be thrown up in the vicinity of the town. The manner in which this business terminated will be stated in its proper place. It will therefore only be necessary to say that this was the King of Ashantee's complaint.

Lieutenant-Colonel Denham, who had been appointed lieutenant-governor of Sierra Leone, sent Major Ricketts back to Cape Coast, in consequence of His Majesty's government having approved of his measures in carrying into effect their instructions to obtain a peace with Ashantee, and to complete the arrangements which Lieutenant-Colonel Lumley had left unfinished, in consequence of some representations made to the government, which he thought might be the means of retaining the charge of the forts.

Major Ricketts returned to Cape Coast on the 5th of June, and having organized a very respectable paid militia, consisting of men of colour, who had served in the Royal African corps, officered by the merchants, and also a volunteer company, composed of the most respectable inhabitants of the town, transferred the charge of the castle and the fort at Accra, together with all the stores that remained in them, to the merchants on the 25th of June.

Major Ricketts, agreeably to the wishes of His Majesty's government to procure a peace with the Ashantees if possible, and nothing having been heard from Coomassie since Captain Kingston wrote to the king, had shortly after his arrival, despatched a man with the following written message to him,

Cape Coast Castle, 14th of June, 1828. Major Ricketts acquaints the King of Ashantee that he has returned to Cape Coast as governor. That he is sorry to find peace has not yet been concluded between the English and Ashantees. Before he left the Gold Coast, from what had been done, he expected the peace would have been settled in a few weeks, but it is now six months since the first messengers returned to Coomassie. There is a vessel about to sail for England, and the governor wishes to know what the King of Ashantee intends to do, that he may acquaint the king of England therewith. The governor of the Cape Coast wishes the King of Ashantee well.

Major Ricketts also wrote privately to Buckman, one of the messengers from Cape Coast, to use his endeavours to get the four thousand ounces of gold, but that if he found there was no chance of succeeding, he was to get as much as he could, and take a bond for the balance payable by instalments; also to acquaint the King of Ashantee, that gold trinkets and *aggery* beads[1] would be accepted. To this message the following letters, which are given in the style in which they were written, were subsequently received from Carr and Buckman.

Coomassie, July 4th, 1628.

Sir,

I beg the honour to acknowledge you letter of the 14th of last month, and which I beg to say, that I accordingly acted the same. I beg further to inform you what has befallen on us. On the second this month, the king and his people assembled and called us, and when we went, they made us repeat the message again. On which all the chiefs and king swore that they will not give a farthing now, because there was a deserter run from Assin, belonging Takoodoom, named Appea, came and told

---

1. These beads are as valuable as gold in the estimation of the natives, and are supposed to have been introduced into the country in former ages for the purchase of slaves. They are generally found under ground, from which it is presumed they must have been used to decorate persons of consequence in former times when interred. To this day the natives keep up this ancient custom of burying their dead with as much pomp as the family of the deceased can afford. These beads are so greatly prized, that the natives do not think themselves sufficiently fine on great festivals and public occasions, unless decorated with some of them. They are the brightest jewels of the country, are very rare, and some traders to the coast endeavour to get similar ones manufactured, and although the imitation is exceedingly good, yet the natives are such great connoisseurs that they immediately discern the difference.

them that it not good palaver we settling with them, because after we got this demand, the same all allies will come and get more by separate. The king himself shook our hands, and told us that as he has found this *palaver* being false, which he thought whites his master, and could not fight them; and as their allies people are going to destroy Elmina, he would not let us come till if you wants a good palaver, having sent Achampong at Elmina back and some of his family at Accra, or Achampong, messenger that will prove as good palaver, then he will send us back, because when we came at first he gave us two prisoners, and we send to Cape Coast, but what we brought in place of them not good ones as theirs; he said also, that if he had mind to kill us, he would before now, but he will not hurt us till the demanded messenger of Elmina or others come, the same he will send us back finely.

He has put Assin's messenger in close confinement, and also Joe Aggery's; the Assins, he said, he punishing them for some time because three of them only have twenty of his women, which none of the women alive now, but all killed; but as King Aggerys, he said, if they let him loose, he will run away, or will give us bad head; but as for me and Mr. Carr, and the last messengers and our boys, are in prison at large, but not in close confinement. He said also, that the proposals for peace are not whites but from blacks, but if whites will let him make peace with them, as they are his masters, then to see and settle the Elmina palaver, and to get the messengers, or those as he said, then he will make the peace, and send us Cape Coast safely.

He said, as white men his masters, that was the reason when he caught late Mr. Williams in war at Samacow, he returned him back through the Dutch governor, but they know that all whites are same and of his masters do him the same favour, then he would know and as certificate that it is good peace they making with him; however, he will never fight with whites, but if white men say they will fight with him on account of the blacks, he will never come as he done before, but he will stop on his own dominions.

 I have the honour to be, Sir,
  Your most obedient humble servant,
          John Buckman.

Coomassie, Saturday, July 12th, 1828.

Sir,

I beg the honour to enclose you this letter. The king called us yesterday, about two o'clock in the afternoon, in his palace, because we make application to him to give us messengers for conveyance. The king gave ours four reasons; first, that when caught late Mr. Williams at Samacow, he returned him without ransom: second, that when we came here he gave one white man and one coloured man, and what he requested you did not grant him, (that was his families,) but sent some unknown persons: third, that we come and he received us, and content to make peace; but now a deserter has come and informed him that your allies are going to kill his messengers at Elmina, therefore, if he did grant the security of peace, the same way turning to him as an enemy: fourth, that King of England he know that he was conqueror of all European kingdoms, and the King of Ashantee was the same before on all blacks, and whenever he fights and conquers, if be that the people give up to serve and make peace with him, he was to bid a great amount that he like; but after having seen that the people truly making good peace through their fidelities, these then he uses to reduce some off, but they said that nothing will be reduced off; that shews that it was not good peace, but still reckon him as an enemy.

Even if the amount was ten thousand ounces of gold bidden, and it reduced to eight thousand ounces, he would yield it; but this shews treachery ,and not good friendly peace hereafter; therefore, he rather blow up once, if white men his masters mean to come over and fight with him, but as himself, he will never come again, and he is very sorry that he is the king of England servant too, and now he has cast him away yielding up for peace, but still forcing him, and going to kill his messengers at Elmina.

I beg leave, further, what I would not fail to inform your command, that there was some Assins came for as his dominions, River Pra side within, some have already made houses and villages, when king heard it, send and brought them from the fifth of this present month to yesterday, sometimes ten, sometimes twenty, which he never forgave them, but kills; we made enquire for that purpose, and was said that they got some families at Adansay, and mean already to come on this king's side, and he did not admit them because they were great rogues in the *palaver*, that might be true, because the last messengers send to me told me, that while he was coming, he was informed that some Assins have run away from our territory, and come this king's side: he said he is ready to make his oath, if required of him. The king said, that if on return of this messenger he brings what he requested, that will shew that you will give him good peace.

 I have the honour to be. Sir,
   Your most obedient, humble servant,
           John Buckman.

      Coomassie, Saturday, July 12th ,1828.

Honoured Sir,

I have the honour to inform you the King of Ashantee's intention about the peace. On Wednesday, the 2nd of this, he assembled all his people to market place, and called us to hear his intention. He told us our master sent us here for peace, but he find that was false, but that was not because he find all what answer he gets from Cape Coast do not agree with white men's affair; in the first place, there is a demand for four thousand ounces of gold for the security of peace, two hostages royal families, and deliver what prisoners he had, will he send one white man and one coloured man, and requested that there was some of his families are at Accra, and if my master wished, for good peace, for to send them to him, and he will see to comply to peace.

My master did not sent them, but send some other men in room of them, and still demanded the said four thousand ounces of gold, and, if he did not sent that, he must let it alone; this white man reply for instance, when he fought the action with late Sir Charles, he did gain the victory over him, and as soon as he did know that there was officer taken by his men, he directly sent him to the whites, and demanded peace from them without any money, only he wished for the delivery of his deserters; and when the whites will not do it, he let Mr. Williams remained, and he thought he would do him the same favour, but he find that was black people's doings, and also there was Assin man come from Cape Coast, he told him that all your allies are going Elmina to take his messengers from them to destroy, and that on that account, he must keep us here, until he get them from Elmina before he can let us go to Cape Coast; he has kept Assin messengers in close confinement with King Aggerys, also intended until he get his families and messengers here, before we can come away.

He says, in his great doubt, he is the person that conquer all the black on this Gold Coast, when he comes to make peace with them, he impose an heavy sum first, and after they depreciate to him in manner as he did to us, he always reduce the sum to one half or one third, and receive them into friendship, and that is not the case now at present, so that he find that what demand my master made, does not seem he as ever will take him in friendship again.

I have the honour to be, &c. &c.

John Carr.

Braman, Kma's Plantation,
Friday 18th July, 1828.

Sir,

We beg the honour to enclose you our last letter. The king called us to his plantation, and told us that this day is a day he would let our messenger despatch, also he told us, that he have no war at all with whites because they are his masters, and would not say so; that, he would not give any security, but it was a messenger sent from Assin, that whether he gives the demand or not, they will come to his country and fight with him, so he said on account of giving the security was to save his country; but now as they says they will come and fight with him, he rather let it alone; also, that they are going to destroy his messengers of Elmina; he did not hide the person who sent to tell him so, name Obel Qran, who we know ourselves.

King has murdered the Assins messengers; we did not fail of asking him about it, he said on account of the abovementioned man's message, and also when they come made fornication with his chief's wife, and still that calling him ill names and challenging him, which custom is not to be excused in this country, so he killed them, but he could not forget them until the peace has been concluded, because they wants to come here and to give some story, and inform there, and also from there to inform here, so that he should not never make peace with you, therefore he would not permit them now, till the peace has been concluded, he still begs that if you send his demand he would make the peace, but you must not mind the Assins, which is to prove one running from there to him."

We are, &c.

John Car,
John Buckman.

P. S. King has released King Aggery's messengers.

Major Ricketts endeavoured by all the measures in his power to persuade the natives to break up their camp near Elmina, and to allow him to make up the differences between them, and the people of that place. The major himself went to Elmina for that purpose, and the native chiefs of that town and the Ashantees who were there assembled in the hall of the castle with the governor. They appeared willing to arrange matters in the manner proposed, which was to meet on the lines, between Cape Coast and Elmina, and there to become friends, and each party to bind themselves in their country way, to keep so, and act together should the Ashantees ever again visit the coast in an hostile manner. The Elminas agreed that this would be the best way of securing tranquillity on the Gold Coast, and the only objection they started was, the contemptible opinion they have of the Fantees, who they said were not trustworthy, and would probably be the first to join the Ashantees should they come down again.

They would, however, have been happy to unite with the Cape Coast natives in mutual assistance in repelling the invasion of either place; but on this being communicated to the allies, they gave evasive answers, and said they knew the Elminas too well to put faith in any of their engagements. The Cape Coast people, though closely connected with the Elminas by family ties, being led away by other natives, also shewed an unwillingness to agree to the union proposed without the allies, stating that as they had been the chief means of bringing them over from the Ashantees to the British cause, they could not separate themselves from them.

Had the arrangements which were first agreed upon by the governors of Danish Accra and Elmina, and the commandant of Cape Coast, namely, for all the chiefs to be present when the Ashantee messengers received their answer, and to desire them to acquaint the king that they were determined to unite against him should he again attempt to disturb the Coast, there is little doubt but peace would have been concluded, but owing to some difference which occurred after

Lieutenant-Colonel Lumley arrived, this was not effected, and the natives seeing that the king's government had withdrawn from the coast, and many of them having been deprived of the monthly allowance which they had officially enjoyed, shewed little attention to what was said to them, and consulted among themselves on the affairs of the country, and whatever they agreed upon they invariably followed.

Major Ricketts, in consequence of the death of Lieutenant-Colonel Lumley, who had again succeeded to the government of Sierra Leone, on the demise of Lieutenant-Colonel Denham, having to go to Sierra Leone to assume the government which had devolved upon him, and there being no prospect of an early accommodation with the King of Ashantee, whose power having been very considerably reduced by his late defeats, and from the circumstance of all the natives from Appalonia to beyond the River Volta, and from the sea coast to the borders of Ashantee, having joined in the war against him, (most of them had been previously considered as his subjects, paid him tribute and assisted him in his wars) there was not, in consequence, much to be apprehended from him; he therefore departed from Cape Coast for Sierra Leone on the 20th of September, taking with him the few remaining persons of the garrison, nearly the whole of whom had previously been sent to Sierra Leone by order of Sir Neil Campbell, and to Ferdinando Po, by Lieutenant-Colonel Lumley, and others transferred to the militia left to garrison the forts under the merchants, and leaving Mr. Jackson, the oldest merchant on the coast, in command.

Sometime after the natives hostile to those of Elmina, having assembled a considerable force, amongst whom were those of Cape Coast, who had professed to observe a strict neutrality in this affair, attacked the town of Elmina, and were driven back with considerable loss, the canon of the fortifications and field pieces having been brought to bear upon them. This defeat caused the whole of them to disperse, and they have remained ever since perfectly quiet.

The Ashantees since their defeat at Dodoowah, have not shown any hostile intentions; and it is said that notwithstanding the prohibited intercourse with them by the native chiefs, a considerable trade is still carried on by smuggling. The Ashantees trade now principally to Assannee, which is situated on the sea coast, considerably to windward of Cape Coast. The merchants are allowed four thousand pounds *per annum* for maintaining and garrisoning the forts at Cape Coast and Accra, which although they have the whole management of the affairs, are still considered dependencies on Sierra Leone.

The negotiations remained in this unsettled state until the month of April, 1831, when the King of Ashantee sent a son and a nephew of his as hostages, to be educated at Cape Coast Castle, accompanied with six hundred ounces of gold to be lodged there as a security for his future good conduct towards the British, Dutch and Danes. Thus terminated these disastrous disputes which had disturbed the country for a period of nearly ten years.

NOTES.

Major de Richelieu, governor in chief of His Danish Majesty's settlements on the Gold Coast, who arrived in the country shortly subsequent to Sir Charles MacCarthy's death, shewed much respect and friendship for our government, by taking an active part in the war. He immediately, on assuming his government, sent all the force he could collect to our aid, and assembled another strong force to proceed through Akim, commanded by himself, towards Ashantee, with a view of diverting the enemy from the coast. The force which arrived from Accra so opportunely at Cape Coast, and assisted in the defeat of the Ashantees on the 11th of July, was partly composed of the Danish Accras and other natives, under the flag of that nation, collected and sent up by Governor Richelieu, who also forwarded some soldiers with an officer, Captain Peloson.

The killed and wounded in this engagement were—Second West India regiment, 3 rank and file wounded. Royal African corps, Lieutenant Swanzy, killed. Militia, 1 rank and file killed, 5 rank and file wounded. Unorganised armed native force, 102 rank and file killed, 410 rank and file wounded. Lieutenant Swanzy was a very promising young officer. He was, as has already been stated, wounded at Dunquah, on the 22nd of February.

The Battle of Dodoowah took place on the 7th of August, 1826.

The head taken there, and supposed to be Sir Charles MacCarthy's, was stated by the man of colour, a returned prisoner from Coomassie, as mentioned, to be that of Tooto Quamina, late King of Ashantee.

BRIEF VIEW OF THE PRESENT STATE OF THE COLONY
OF SIERRA LEONE

CHAPTER 1

Succession of Governors

In the preceding narrative I have described, as well as my brief notes would admit, the various negotiations and battles with the Ashantees, in which it was my lot to be employed; and as the colony of Sierra Leone has excited a great share of public interest, whilst from a diversity of opinions it has been variously represented, I shall endeavour to give a correct account of its present state, and of its inhabitants.

It was my lot to witness, during the period of my service on the coast, the arrival and premature decease of five successive governors; viz. Sir Charles MacCarthy, Major-General Turner, General Sir Neil Campbell, Lieutenant-Colonel Denham, and lastly, Lieutenant-Colonel Lumley; whom I had the honour to succeed in the government. Of the unhappy and cruel fate of Sir Charles MacCarthy, I have already spoken in the preceding narrative.

Major-General Turner arrived in the colony in February, 1825. His death was caused by his unremitting exertions up the River Sherbro, where he fought several actions with the natives and others engaged in the slave trade; after which he returned to Sierra Leone in a bad state of health, and died in March, 1826.

General Sir Neil Campbell arrived in the colony in August, 1826, and sailed shortly after for the Gold Coast; from whence he returned and was seized with sickness in November following. Having recovered, he proceeded to the Gambia, and returned in a short time in better health; but soon after fell sick again, and died in August, 1827.

Colonel Lumley arrived in the colony at the same time with Sir Neil Campbell, and after the death of that officer, assumed the government, and in about six weeks proceeded to the Gold Coast, from whence he returned in April, 1828, when he was superseded by Lieutenant-Colonel Denham, upon whose decease, he again assumed the government, and died in August, 1828.

I first became acquainted with Colonel Denham at British Accra, in the month of January, 1828, where he had arrived from Sierra Leone. His celebrity as an African traveller had already excited a high degree of interest in his favour, and upon his landing he was received with every mark of respect.

Shortly after, we visited the Danish castle "Christianburg" together, and were received by the governor with much civility; after which Colonel Denham embarked on board the *Sybill*, Commodore Collier, and I, on board a transport for Fernandez Po. After remaining there several days. Colonel Denham sailed again with that officer, and returned to Freetown, in the *Plumper* brig of war, after a long passage, much straightened for provisions and water, where I had preceded him nearly a month. He had at this time been upwards of twelve months the superintendant of the liberated Africans, and, as I had served in the different settlements on the coast for nearly eleven years, and had had much intercourse with the natives, he seemed desirous of obtaining whatever information it was in my power to give, and I feel persuaded that the general coincidence of our opinions was a source of mutual satisfaction.

His exertions whilst he superintended the liberated Africans in their villages, and also his judicious plans and exertions for the short time he was governor, were highly beneficial and useful, and would no doubt have produced in time the most desirable effects. He had whilst in the discharge of his arduous duty adopted an excellent plan of locating the people along , the roads, by giving each individual a certain portion of land adjoining his own house, which plan I also followed, conceiving it to be the most advantageous that could be suggested, and the most probable means by which the colony could be effectually improved. He had heard of his appointment, and his reception at Freetown was highly gratifying to his feelings, being met on landing, by a body of the inhabitants, who escorted him to the government house.

After he was sworn in, he dispatched me back to the Gold Coast to complete the arrangements that had been previously ordered by government, and very shortly after this he died of the Sierra Leone fever, to the great regret of all classes of those who were able to. appreciate his talents and virtues. He survived the first attack only about nine days. By this unfortunate event the government again devolved upon Colonel Lumley, but he also soon afterwards fell a victim to the climate. I then assumed the government, which, in consequence of ill health, I was obliged reluctantly to relinquish and return to England, after having served in various capacities on that coast, during the period already mentioned.

Sierra Leone is a peninsula, very mountainous, and so named it is presumed by the Portuguese, from the roaring of the thunder through the valleys on the approach and at the termination of the rainy season, resembling that of a lion. It is situated in latitude 8 deg. 30 min. north, and 13 deg. 43 min. west longitude, and was transferred from the African company in 1808, to His Majesty's government.

The scenery upon drawing near the colony from the sea is picturesque, and in sailing along the land (which is on the right) towards the harbour, the verdure of the woods is delightful, being partly composed of the beautiful palm tree, and here and there on the hills are seen cultivated spots with some good sized houses, and the barracks as the country occasionally opens, until anchored in front of Freetown, which has a picturesque appearance, especially if viewed at a distance from the shore, many of the houses being built on a gentle declivity from Fort Thornton, close to which the old barracks stand: the three new barracks and hospital have a fine effect from the sea: the former, built of bricks, with joists and posts of iron, and slated roofs, are situated on a considerable eminence at a short distance in the rear of Fort Thornton. The two former contain each one hundred and seventy persons, and the other a proportionate number of officers.

The hospital is a very good one; it is situated half way between the old and new barracks and at the foot of the ascent to the latter.

The Bullom shore, on the left whilst making for the harbour, is low land, and some parts are often overflowed during the rains, and about ten miles north-east from Freetown, across to Leopold Island, the most leeward point of the Bullom shore; close to which, on the main land, resides Delamoody, a very intelligent native chief, and a man of great influence among the surrounding native tribes. On landing at Freetown, a stranger is not a little surprised to behold a place so far superior to what he had been induced to expect; and if he should arrive in the *hermitan* season, when resident Europeans are generally in better health than at other periods of the year, from its salubrious effects, he will be saluted with an agreeable smell, similar to that of new hay, and will wonder how it was possible the place could be so unhealthy as represented; but on the approach of the rainy season, his wonder begins to cease.

The *hermitan* is a very dry easterly wind, which, in a few days, dries up all vegetation, except trees; it sets in about December, and continues at intervals for several days together: such is the nature of the *hermitan*, that the flooring of the houses, window shutters, and other wood work, shrink and separate more than an inch asunder; the glass is broken, and the furniture is warped, but at the approach of the rains, the open seams gradually close again.

After the absence of rain for many months, the parched surface of the earth, all its vegetation, except trees, having been dried up by the *hermitan*, and then scorched by the intense heat of a tropical sun, is suddenly covered with verdure. The day after the first shower, the force of vegetation is so great, that the face of nature is completely changed, and it may literally be said that the grass and weeds may be seen to grow; yet, however strange it may appear, although these, as well as the indigo plant, grow spontaneously everywhere, new land will not satisfactorily produce the usual articles of consumption for three successive years, and some land will not even yield the second year. The rainy season is preceded by dry tornados, which towards the latter end of May are accompanied by rain; they last generally for about an hour, sometimes not so long. They very much resemble the hurricanes in the West Indies, but are not so furious; they vary from south-east to north-east. A dark cloud in the eastern horizon foretells the approach of a tornado; it advances, accompanied by tremendous thunder and vivid flashes of lightning, which at first are distant and faint, until the whole heavens gradually become obscured by one black cloud.

It frequently happens that from the quarter opposite to that where the cloud first appears, there previously arises a breeze, which dies away, as the tornado gathers; the atmosphere then becomes very sultry, and the tornado advances, with a great rush of wind, bursts, sweeping before it (if no rain has previously fallen) immense clouds of dust. The wet tornados are succeeded by a beautifully serene sky, and the air is greatly refreshed; the frame becomes invigorated, and the mind more cheerful. As the rainy season advances, the tornados gradually cease, and are succeeded by almost constant heavy rains. At the termination of the rains, the tornados again make their appearance, becoming weaker as the dry season approaches, until they cease altogether.

At intervals during the day in the rainy season, the action of an intensely hot sun on the earth, covered with a luxuriant vegetation, and saturated with moisture, produces a disagreeable sickening smell, which is probably one of the causes of the fever that prevails at this period of the year, as persons recently arrived are generally taken ill in July or August; some, however, have been known to reside in the colony above two years without having been affected by it. If they remain beyond this time, they are certain not to escape much longer, and when at length they take the fever, it generally proves fatal to them. It is considered the more favourable symptoms for a stranger to be seized with the fever soon after his arrival. The havoc which this dreadful disease has made among the Europeans who have gone out, or have been sent to the colony is well known.

On the first arrival of European troops in 1825, they died in greater numbers than at any subsequent period; the cause was attributed much to the incomplete state of the barracks, which had been hastily erected, the materials arriving from England at the same time with the troops, the barracks could not consequently be covered in before the rains. From the want of accommodation on shore, most of the troops were kept on board the transports for some months. After the completion of the barracks, and the walls had become dry, the troops enjoyed better health, but they drank freely, and it was very difficult to keep them sober. This no doubt tended much to bring on sickness among them; the officers died, however, in proportion.

Black troops, well regulated, are the best to garrison the colony, but they should be composed of men from the Gold Coast, as they are better calculated for soldiers than any other natives of the coast of Africa, and they should be enlisted for a limited period, as the idea that they may return to their own country at the expiration of their term, will render them happy and contented. They deserted in great numbers in 1826, when ordered from Cape Coast to Sierra Leone, on account of their entertaining an idea that they would never be allowed to return.

The coast is now garrisoned by three companies of the Royal African corps, consisting of one hundred men each, stationed at Sierra Leone, at the Gambia, and at Fernandez Po; there are also recruiting parties of the 1st and 2nd West India regiments at Sierra Leone. These regiments have been very successful in obtaining recruits among the liberated Africans, from the villages who voluntarily enlist, and cheerfully embark for the West In dies. All the European troops have been sent home, and the whole of the coast is now garrisoned by native soldiers.

I formed and cloathed an excellent militia, well drilled, composed of the youngest of the discharged soldiers having pensions from government, and liberated Africans, who readily joined at the villages of Wellington and York, and officered by European and coloured superintendants of those places.

A militia of Freetown was also in progress of formation, when I departed from the colony, and should these people be encouraged, they will, in all probability, fully answer every purpose required; but it will be always necessary to have a small regular garrison, in order to sustain the military character of the place in the eyes of the natives.

The population of the colony is about twenty-six thousand. Freetown is inhabited by European merchants, who have built houses for their stores and residences. Maroons, Nova Scotians, blacks, (called settlers,) discharged soldiers from the West India regiments, exiles, from Barbadoes, and liberated Africans, who have obtained lots of land in the town. It is well and regularly laid out, and the streets, most of which lately have been properly constructed, are sixty feet wide. Notwithstanding the money which has been expended on public buildings, there are none in the town with the exception of the jail, the barracks, the commissariat, and the buildings of the liberated Africans, that are worthy of the name. The houses, from the destructive nature of the climate, require annual reparation; even iron, unless well painted, will not withstand its effects long. The buildings are erected with a red clay stone, which is found in quarries in the neighbourhood.

A battery to the eastward of the town has lately been repaired and improved. It is the only fortification in the colony, except Fort Thornton, which is in a dilapidated state, and in a bad situation, being nearly in the centre of the town, surrounded by houses. There are a few guns mounted to the westward of the town, close to the buildings of the liberated Africans above-mentioned, which it would be dangerous to fire, in consequence of the ground on which they stand, being undermined by the sea, the concussion might consequently cause it to give way, and thereby injure the buildings; there are also three guns mounted simply on the ground, on King Tom's point, a little farther on, at the entrance of the harbour. The guns of the battery to the eastward cannot reach a vessel until she enters the harbour, and then she might easily get under shelter of the houses that intervene between the battery and the west end of the town. A battery of a few guns, on Cape Sierra Leone, close to which vessels must pass on entering the harbour, would be desirable for the maritime defence of Freetown.

The entrance of the channel of the river is narrow, although it is fifteen miles wide at its mouth; the tides ebb and flow exceedingly strong, and the shoal called the middle ground, which is on the left on going into the harbour, is very steep. The harbour is only accessible in safety with a sea breeze, which sets in between twelve and two in the day, but cannot always be depended upon; as at times it is very weak, and of short duration.

The beach to the westward from False Cape to Cape Shilling, on which the village of Kent is built, is guarded by a surf, which renders it dangerous for a boat to land, and canoes of the country are consequently used along it. The sea beach towards the Sherbro estuary is open and easy for landing, and consequently needs some protection.

For the land defence of the colony against the natives of the continent, a fortification appears necessary near the village of Waterloo, which is only divided from the main land by a small stream of water in the rainy season, when Sierra Leone may be called an island, but the water disappearing in the dry season, it thus becomes a peninsula.

Next to the Europeans, the Maroons are the most respectable class in the colony. Some of these people, as well as the Nova Scotians, have acted as commissioners of requests, and have filled the office of mayor, aldermen, and sheriff. During the government of Sir Charles MacCarthy, they took great pride in these appointments, but latterly they reluctantly accept of any honorary office. A few of them, as well as some of the other people of colour, keep small retail shops of goods and ardent spirits, purchased on credit from the European merchants at auctions, where they pay cash; and some of the Maroons have shops on nearly as large ascale as the Europeans, and import their own goods from England, whence vessels are often sent out to them for a cargo of timber.

They possess a considerable proportion of the houses in Freetown, which are principally built of stone, wood, and shingles, and consist generally of a hall, two bed rooms, and a *piazza* supported by stone pillars, the hall and bed rooms are raised about five feet from the ground on stonework of which the walls also of the houses are built. The under part of the house is used as a store room or cellar. There are other houses of wood built on stone foundations. The merchants' houses are built upon a much larger scale.

In consequence of very high rents being given for lodgings for the officers and other persons in the public service, whilst the public buildings were in the course of construction, the Maroon mechanics, who reaped large profits, were induced to build some better houses than have been mentioned; many of which however have never been finished, owing to the failure of means, and the impossibility of letting them, the public expenditure not long after the commencement of the speculation having been greatly curtailed and the public servants accommodated in government buildings. Houses of a good description are consequently now seen in various parts of the town uninhabited, or unfinished, and falling to decay. The settlers inhabit the eastern part of the town, designated Settlers Town.

These people are inferior to the Maroons in respectability, but have been longer in the colony. Their houses in general are not so good, they are not so industrious, are addicted to drinking, and most of them are of indifferent principles; they have decreased, while the Maroons have increased in number latterly. There has always existed a hostile feeling and jealousy between these people and the Maroons, but which is now slowly subsiding; there are however a few exceptions among them, who are deserving to be classed among the most respectable coloured inhabitants of the colony.

Divine service was formerly performed over the jail, and was well attended by the blacks, but lately in the unfinished new church in the centre of the town, where but few of either Europeans or blacks attend. The latter have erected several places of worship of their own.

The Maroons deserve credit for the neat little chapel they have erected by subscription among themselves. They had formerly a Methodist preacher, whom they procured from England, but like most other Europeans he did not survive long. There is also a respectable Wesleyan chapel in Settler Town, which is well attended, and many other private places of worship for dissenters are in different parts of the town, which are supported by contributions from congregations consisting principally of liberated Africans and discharged soldiers: very few of these can even read, and many of the former hardly understand English; and perhaps the preacher, who may be a discharged soldier, or a liberated African himself scarcely knows his letters, yet they join heartily in singing psalms, which constitutes the principal part of their service.

These latter places are opened at daylight for about an hour, and in the evening from six till eight o'clock: the chanting may be heard at a considerable distance, and their discordant voices are not a little annoying to the Europeans, who happen to reside in the immediate neighbourhood. On the Lord's day the shops are closed and the Sabbath is otherwise religiously observed by the coloured population.

Many persons belonging to the surrounding tribes have taken up their temporary residence in the colony, and the Mahometan religion, which many of them profess, allowing a man to have several wives, is in that respect making much progress. With the exception of the most respectable of the Maroons and Nova Scotians, the native inhabitants have not advanced much in European civilization, not being so refined in this respect as a domestic slave in the West Indies; but they are fond of dress, and newly liberated Africans soon follow their example to the extent of their means.

The Maroons still, (1831), retain a dialect peculiar to them in Jamaica. Some of the Maroon lads, by being employed in the European's shops, improve themselves much, particularly in their writing. They occasionally give parties, at which there are young ladies who figure away in a country dance, copied from the Europeans, some of whom give a ball and supper, but to which none of the males of colour are invited except one individual, a merchant, who is often a guest at the dinner table of the Europeans. In Sir Charles MacCarthy's time the coloured people who by their good conduct became deserving of his notice, were received at his table, and marriage among them was much encouraged.

CHAPTER 2

Commercial Pursuits

The liberated Africans are now supported by government only for six months after liberation in the colony by the mixed-commission courts, at the rate of two pence per day for each adult, and three half-pence per day for children: a piece of cloth sufficiently large to wrap round the body, and a blanket, is given to each individual, or one blanket between two children, on landing. The men are not located until three months after they are received by the liberated official department, being employed on light work during that time for the good of the public. When I assumed the government, I adopted the plan of sending half the newly-arrived African males to clear land and build huts for themselves, and the remainder was kept in Freetown and employed in the manner above stated.

Thus they were provided with houses and provision-grounds when their time of working for the public had expired. During the six months they have also issued to them two shirts and two pair of trowsers each, and when located, provided with implements of agriculture and cooking utensils. The government provide for them as already stated during six months, at the expiration of which they are put on their own resources, and are usually assisted by their own country people until they are well able to maintain themselves.

Some of the men are occasionally apprenticed to the merchants who are engaged in the timber trade up the rivers, and favourable reports have been made of them. They will readily hire themselves, but they require much looking after. Many of them after having resided some time in the colony, acquire a small capital, principally by traffic in European articles. None of these people hire themselves as sailors on board of ships, nor do they serve as boatmen, owing to their incapacity; but a few of them possess canoes, in which they employ the neighbouring natives, and trade to the adjacent rivers with European merchandize, which they exchange for rice, to retail again in Freetown. Some of the discharged soldiers employ themselves also in this manner. This is the kind of occupation which these people like; and as soon as any of them, acquire some capital in another line, they speculate in traffic. Some of them also saw boards, and split shingles, which they sell at Freetown.

The women get married, as they are not allowed to be taken otherwise by the men, almost immediately after being landed. Some of the girls and boys are apprenticed to the inhabitants on liberation, and the remainder sent to school in the villages, where they are supported and cloathed until they are either apprenticed or able to provide for themselves; some of the girls are also disposed of from thence in marriage.

I ordered the boys at school in the villages to cultivate a farm at each place, that they might support and cloath themselves without expense to government, by the sale of arrow root, ginger, and rice, of which they had a good quantity planted, as well as other articles of food when I departed for Europe.

There are seventeen liberated African villages in the colony, *viz.* Regent, Leopold, Gloucester, and Charlotte, in the mountains; Kissey, Wellington, Allen's Town, Hastings, Waterloo, Wilberforce, Murray, Aberdeen, Denham, York, Kent, and two on the Banana islands, *viz.* Dublin and Ricketts. Murray and Aberdeen were recently formed by me, on the right bank of the river, sailing into the harbour; the former about three miles, the latter four miles and a half from Freetown. The land is some of the best in the colony, and they bid fair to equal, if not surpass, many of the villages previously settled. The town and country lots were regularly laid out, houses were built, and the land was planted, before distribution.

At Regent, Leopold, Kissey, Wellington, Hastings, Waterloo, Kent, and York, some small houses of stone and wood, have been erected by the liberated African mechanics, but principally by the discharged pensioned native soldiers, who are located at the five latter places, and a few of whom, as well as some of the liberated Africans, are in possession of comfortable houses in Freetown.

They were also building at Wellington, by subscription among the discharged soldiers, and the liberated Africans, a good sized market, and a chapel of stone, and they wish to have the privilege of appointing their own preacher. At Regent, Leopold, Gloucester, and Kissey, where there are respectable churches built by government, the liberated Africans of these villages, and of others where missionaries are stationed, attend divine service regularly and are neatly dressed on Sundays in the English costume for that purpose; at other times, except on particular occasions, most of them are nearly without clothing. The Missionary Society have lately established schools at Freetown, and at some of the liberated African villages, for the children born in the colony.

By a late regulation entered into with them, the liberated African children are allowed to participate in the benefits arising from these schools. They are conducted on the infantine system, which is admirably calculated for African children. The children who are born in the colony are very much superior in intellect, and in every other respect, to those liberated from slavery, and may be readily distinguished, although their parents may be liberated Africans themselves. If there were other schools to which the boys could be sent as they grow up for further instruction, they might prove very useful in a colony so fatal to European life; but hitherto none of the liberated Africans who have been at school, with the exception of a few employed as teachers by the missionaries, on whose instruction great pains have been bestowed, have benefited much by the schools established by government; but this may have been owing to the want of good teachers, and of a proper system. The schools at Freetown, for boys and girls born in the colony, are well attended by the children of the Maroons, Nova Scotians and others; the teachers are American blacks, who came to settle at the American settlement called Liberia, 6 deg. north latitude and 11 deg. east longitude; but they are not very efficient in their various capacities.

The colony abounds with steep mountains, separated with deep ravines, formed by the rain rushing down the sides of the precipices, which, after, collecting in the valleys, finds its way to the river and to the sea. Bridges have been repeatedly thrown across the ravines, some at considerable expense, and which were considered calculated to stand, but they have all shared the like fate, being soon washed away by the great torrents of water, which frequently bring down large trees. The mountains, when cleared of woods, soon lose much of the superficial soil, which is washed into the valleys by the heavy rains, and thus become nearly destitute, with the exception of small deposits of earth, retained by the irregularity of the rocky surface.

The remainder of the colony is composed of declivities, deep valleys, and plains, comprising a great quantity of flat rock . Some of the hills, as well as a large portion of the country in the vicinity of the old established liberated African villages, are well cleared of the high woods, while in the vicinity of Freetown, where the land belongs to the Maroons and Nova Scotians, much high wood is still standing; and the land is but partially cultivated. The soil, after having been in use two or three years, that which at first was considered the best, will hardly repay the cultivator, in keeping down the grass and weeds which grow up again almost as soon as they are removed; therefore, the same spots are seldom or never cultivated after the first or second year, but are allowed to remain fallow for a few years, before they are again put into requisition, when the brush wood, which has sprung up to a certain height, is cut down and burnt, and manures the land, which is the only means of doing so, and renders it again productive. For this reason, the inhabitants who till the soil have several pieces of ground, which they cultivate alternately, some of which are situated at a distance of several miles from their respective villages.

The articles raised are yams, cocoa, *casada*, a small quantity of rice and Indian corn, pine apples, a few sugar canes, pumpkins, melons, *ochras*, and a few greens. The inhabitants do not grow sufficient rice for their own consumption, and a great quantity is imported for that purpose from the neighbouring countries. There is an abundance of oranges, and a few cocoa nut trees; some coffee trees have also been planted on some of the hills near Freetown by Europeans; but of late they have been entirely neglected. One of these places was first planted by Governor Maxwell, and was purchased from him by the late Sir Charles MacCarthy, who built a good house upon it. It lately belonged to Mr. Kenneth Macauly, since deceased.

Some of the coffee trees appeared healthy,, and produced tolerably well. The coffee collected was esteemed very excellent, and resembled Mocha coffee in appearance and taste. In clearing the woods about Wellington some years ago, a considerable number of coffee trees of great height were discovered, and some of the berries on them being collected at the time, proved to be real coffee; but the villagers, not being aware of the utility of the trees, cut them down in clearing the woods.

During the period that I administered the government, I gave directions for the liberated Africans to plant on their farms a certain number of coffee and ginger plants, which latter thrives well in some parts of the colony, as does also arrow root; and I encouraged the discharged pensioned soldiers in the villages, who were cultivators, as far as it was possible, by supplying them with ginger for planting. Whether the cultivation of these articles have been persevered in is doubtful, from the difficulty which they experienced in disposing of some small quantity which they had reared, and the low price obtained for ginger and arrow root from the merchants, who would give only goods in payment. It was my plan to promote this kind of cultivation by finding a market in England, and I hoped for the assistance of the friends of the colony at home, as many of them had expressed their willingness to purchase all the ginger that might be raised by these people.

As a further stimulus to the colonist, an Agricultural Society was formed, and a tract of about one hundred acres of the best land was cleared and planted with corn, white rice, ginger, coffee and yams. It looked well, and was in a state of great forwardness when I departed for England; but it is apprehended that it has, like many other plans commenced for the improvement of the colony, been neglected. Even when it was going on prosperously, few of the subscribers ever went to look at it: so indifferent were they to its success, that some of them sold their shares for half the sum which they had paid for them. No well-followed up examples in these respects have ever been offered to the liberated Africans, nor encouragement given to them. The lands which were given to the Maroons and Nova Scotians on their arrival in this colony, with few exceptions, although situated in the immediate vicinity of Freetown, have been only partially cleared of the woods. They state, in excuse, that the land is too unproductive, but in appearance it is equally as good as at the two villages already mentioned, as having been formed by me, which is considered as some of the best in the colony.

The stock reared in the colony, are a few cows and bullocks, some pigs, fowls, and ducks. The supplies for the colony and shipping are chiefly obtained from the Mandingoes and Foulahs, who bring them from the interior of the continent, and by the neighbouring natives. The market place in Freetown is a large unfinished brick building, erected by government for the purpose, and the upper part is intended for a court house. It is well supplied with fresh meat, poultry, rice, vegetables, and fruit; the latter articles by the natives of the neighbouring shores, and by the liberated Africans. The market is held from day light in the morning till four o'clock in the afternoon, every day except Sunday. A tax which I laid on the articles and animals exposed for sale in the market, was calculated to produce nearly seven hundred pounds a year; and in consequence of this regulation the market became much more frequented, although at first it was not liked by the natives.

It is astonishing to see some of the market people, who for the want of room, or in preference, sit outside of the building the whole of the day without any covering on their heads, or perhaps without any cloathing at all, except a piece of cloth tied round their bodies, exposed to a vertical sun, which almost strikes a European to the ground, and would blister his skin if exposed to it only for a short time. The exports from the colony are timber, rice, occasionally to the West Indies, palm oil, some camwood, a small quantity of bees-wax, and now and then some gold.

The timber is generally teak, which is obtained at a considerable distance up the branches of the Sierra Leone River, which are called Bunce, Rokel, Port Logo, and Mahara Rivers; these are intersected by numerous creeks, on the banks of which the timber is felled and squared by the natives themselves, and with cork wood floated by them to the factories established by the European merchants on these streams, where it is purchased with goods and shipped for England.

In consequence of the timber of these places becoming scarce, and likely to be shortly exhausted altogether, the merchants have also established factories at the Rivers Furicaria and Scarces, from thirty to forty miles to the northward of Sierra Leone. The entrances into these rivers were dangerous, but their mouths having been surveyed lately, ships now go in and load with greater facility. The present great demand for the timber arises in consequence of a contract by some persons in England to supply government with a certain number of loads of it, by a given period for ship building.

The palm oil and camwood are obtained from the neighbouring rivers, and the wax and gold brought by some of the inland natives, with whom at one time a hope was entertained that a considerable trade might be established, as they came oftener to the colony with their merchandize owing to considerable presents having been made to their chiefs by the government; this not being continued of late, and the Rio Pongas and Rio Nunez being much nearer to them, where they can dispose of slaves, they generally go there, and visit Sierra Leone only, when induced through interest made with them by the merchants.

Another circumstance which operates against their intercourse with the colony is, the expense which they incur for canoes to convey them and their merchandise from the places where they are obliged to proceed by water to the colony, which are distant from forty to one hundred miles up the rivers. Horses are obtained from Senegal and the Gambia, but they might be reared in the colony. A gig can be driven from Freetown through the village of Kissey to Wellington, and the road is nearly level the whole way, and those who keep horses and vehicles ride out in the mornings but generally in the evenings during the dry season of the year round Furrah Bay, about a mile from the town. All the other roads are steep and rocky, and are therefore with difficulty traversed with horses.

The roads are repaired once a year, shortly after the rains, by the liberated Africans in the villages. Unless some method should be devised to give employment to the greatly increasing population caused by the emancipation of slaves, who are almost daily arriving, now that the public expenditure has declined comparatively to nothing, it is probable the liberated Africans will relapse from their present state of civilization into their former habits and customs. There was evidently such a tendency when I quitted the colony.

The liberated Africans of the Pacongo nation, with the exception of a very few of them, will not remain in the villages, but secret themselves in the woods, whence they occasionally emerge for plunder. These are cannibals; and one of them was taken not very long since with a human hand in his wallet, and even some of the discharged soldiers have a propensity to seclude themselves in the bushes, where they build huts. The most intelligent among the liberated Africans are the Accoos, who are of a warlike tribe: they have already given some trouble, and as they are increasing considerably in number, it is not improbable they may, at no distant period, cause much alarm. It is however generally considered that the Maroons, Nova Scotians, and soldier pensioners, with the other liberated Africans, are a sufficient check upon them, as well as upon each other, for the peace of the colony, which must in time be inhabited by one people only, namely, their descendants.

A great number of men and women from the neighbouring countries take up their residence in the suburbs of the town, the greater part of them without permission from the proper authorities. Some of these are criminals, who have fled from the justice of their own country, and who furnish a bad example to the liberated people by the evil practices which they introduce with them. Some of them, after a short residence in the colonies, instigated a war in the neighbourhood, and nearly involved the colony in it. The merchants were much interrupted by it in their timber and other trade. These persons dance and sing in their country fashion.

The Maroons born in the colony dance to the *gumbia* (drum) to which they sing and keep time by clapping their hands together. This custom was introduced by the original Maroons from Jamaica. Those who are still in existence speak of their former residence with fond remembrances and sigh to return to it. There are a number of *kroomen* generally at Sierra Leone. They come from about Cape Palmas to seek employment in the colony and on board the ships of war and merchant vessels. They are industrious, and being active and strong, are always employed in preference to the other natives. They inhabit a small nest of huts near Freetown.

As soon as a *krooman* has laid by as much money as he thinks will enable him to appear in his own country as a person of consequence, he purchases goods, which he takes with him home, and after his wealth has been exhausted, he returns to seek for more. Numbers of them enter the navy for a period of three years. Each vessel is allowed to take a number proportioned to her rating, and they receive about the same pay as the white seamen, and also share in prize money. They have been of infinite use in preserving the lives of our sailors by going generally in the boats in their stead.

The Banana islands, dependencies of Sierra Leone, about thirty miles to the southward and westward of Freetown, and two miles across from the village of Kent, are very beautiful and the soil is excellent. The land has been mostly laid out by the surveyor in town and country lots, and each person inhabiting the islands possesses one of each, and in consequence of the country lots being properly cultivated, the islands look exceedingly fine, just about the close of the rainy season, when the crops are nearly ready to reap. Mr. Campbell, who had been upwards of fourteen years in the colony, part of which time had been spent in the navy and on board the Colonial vessel, which captured many slaves, and was sent to the Bananas, had a plantation of coffee, ginger, and other things in which he took a great deal of interest. To his exertions this prosperous state of the islands must be attributed. There is a very good house upon one of them which was commenced by Sir Charles MacCarthy and subsequently completed by me.

The Bananas are decidedly the most healthy of our possessions in Africa, and if the capital of Sierra Leone, which was chosen principally for the harbour, it being a very good one, had been formed at the place, now occupied by the village of Ricketts, where there is an excellent anchorage for ships of any class, and it is evident by the good state of health which the Europeans have enjoyed there, that many valuable lives might have been saved. There are other dependencies of Sierra Leone called the Isles de Loss, where good barracks and other buildings were erected at a very great expense, but which are now falling to decay, the place having been abandoned; there are some pensioned soldiers, who have been settled on the most fertile of the islands still remaining there. Two of these islands, *viz*. Tamara and Factory, are said to be tolerably healthy, but are by no means comparable in that respect to the Bananas.

On the other island, designated Crawford's, which is very small and exceedingly rocky, the barracks were built, and it proved fatal to many of the European troops, recruits of the African Colonial corps, whom Major-General Turner had brought from England with him, and were sent there on account of its being considered more healthy than Sierra Leone.

These islands were taken possession of to prevent the Americans forming a settlement there, as was reported to have been their intention. If they had effected this purpose, it would have interfered materially with the trade of Sierra Leone. Two Europeans traders still have factories on these islands, and a considerable merchant, who is a Maroon, has formed a settlement on an island called Mattercong, about thirty miles from Sierra Leone, which he is cultivating, the soil being superior to that of the colony.

When liberated Africans were first located at Sierra Leone, if a system like the following had been adopted and pursued, it is probable that they would now have been attached to the soil, and better able to provide for themselves and children; *viz*. Select the best land, and make all the males capable of labour work in a body in clearing and planting articles for their own use, besides coffee and other exportable produce; this being accomplished, apportion the land out to them, building a house on each farm, which they should be compelled to keep in order, on penalty of forfeiting their settlement. At present, except those who are tied to the villages by possessing good houses in them, the liberated Africans move from place to place as their fancy leads them, and as no regular allotment until lately had been given to them, they sit down as they call it wherever they like. Ideas of perfect liberty have too soon been given to these people considering their utter ignorance. If one of them were now asked why he does not repair his house, clean his farm, mend his fence, or put on better clothes, he replies, "that king no give him work this time, and that he can do no more than burn bush and plant little *cassada* for yam" (to eat.)

The trade in slaves is carried to a greater extent than formerly, in the neighbouring rivers; the vessels that frequent them carry for this purpose Spanish dollars and *doubloons*, which subsequently find their way to Sierra Leone for goods. Many of the liberated Africans have been enticed from the colony, and others kidnapped by the vagabonds already mentioned who reside in the suburbs of Freetown: they are resold as slaves; some of them after a few months have been recaptured in slave vessels, and brought back to the colony to be liberated. The numerous creeks in the immediate vicinity of Sierra Leone, which communicate with the rivers, afford great facility for carrying them off. I had an inspection of the liberated African apprentices shortly after I assumed the government, but there were not so many unaccounted for as was anticipated.

It appears to be the intention of government to remove the mixed commissioned court to Fernandez Po, and to fill up the necessary establishment of the government at Sierra Leone with coloured people, whom it would be necessary to procure from foreign parts, as there are few people of colour competent to fill any important government office; and should the colony be abandoned by government, the slave trade will immediately revive: it is at present carried on secretly by some of the unprincipled black population, but in general the trade is abhorred by them.

These are no doubt wise measures, inasmuch as the misery of the poor slaves consequent on their voyage up, if taken to any distance to leeward, is very much aggravated. Sometimes the vessels captured in the bight of Benin and Biafra, where or near to which by far the greater portion of the slaves are taken, are six weeks, and often longer, on their passage, on account of an easterly current; but on the approach of the periodical rains, the passage is made in much less time, from the winds inclining to the north east. Vessels going up to Sierra Leone from these places are, in consequence of a strong current which runs to the eastward, compelled to go sometimes two degrees southward of the line, (which is at times attended with great difficulty,) in order to get the north east wind, before which they bear away for Sierra Leone with flowing sails.

The winds on the coast are about south-west. Numerous deaths occur among the slaves on their passage, from its tedious length; and sometimes they are much straightened for provisions and water. The slave vessels have been known to be from two months to eleven weeks on their passage up the coast. The male slaves are generally secured by the slave traders with irons between decks, but the women are seldom confined, and are kept in a separate part of the ship, and small parties are allowed to come upon deck in rotation.

The Portuguese and Spaniards impress on the minds of the slaves that the English are anxious to destroy them; in consequence of which the poor creatures are just after capture much dejected; but as they are generally immediately released from their confinement and every possible attention paid to them, they soon become cheerful, and although totally unacquainted with one another's language, shortly become familiarised by signs or motions, and when anchored in Freetown harbour, awaiting their adjudication, their countrymen located in the colony visit them, and from being acquainted with their approaching delivery, they indulge in merriment and pleasure. Should there be any disease among the slaves on board the ships, they are landed as soon as the necessary legal forms are gone through. Many of these poor creatures arrive in such a deplorable state from want and disease, that it is difficult to preserve their lives.

It is really shocking to humanity to see a cargo of children arrive sometimes mere skeletons, in a complete state of exhaustion. The small pox and measles often break out on board the slave vessels, as well as the opthalmia. Slaves are purchased from the natives on an average for about four pounds each, and are paid for in gunpowder, arms, tobacco, ardent spirits, &c. Those taken in the latitude of Sierra Leone, might reach Fernandez Po in fifteen or twenty days.

The last dreadful epidemic fever, in 1829, was evidently brought to Sierra Leone, as will appear by the following account. About the 1st of May, 1829, a new description of fever broke out among the inhabitants of Freetown, and the shipping lying in the harbour. Previous to which, the only casualty that had for some time occurred amongst the Europeans, was the death of a young writer in the secretary's office, who died of a first attack of the fever common to this part of Africa. The casualties among the coloured people located in Freetown were very limited, and chiefly confined to those well advanced in years.

The crews of the merchant vessels visiting the colony for timber, were, (excepting one or two that were not properly attended to,) up to this period healthy, but from, this time to September, the oldest European residents, including Mr. Kenneth Macauley, who had been nearly twenty years in the colony, and Mr. Reffell, who had been above fourteen, and many native settlers in Freetown, fell victims to this disease, which was rapidly destroying the crews of the shipping. Of twenty *kroomen* landed from His Majesty's ship *Eden*, eight died of this disease; and these people, the most hardy on the coast, died on an average of one a day, since this fever appeared, although previously healthy.

The fever which carried off so many of the European troops on the Gold Coast in 1824, was in all probability similar to this. This disease was, with a very few exceptions among the merchant seamen, unknown at Sierra Leone since the year 1823, when it broke out on board the *Caroline*, a merchant ship from the Mediterranean, and spread from her, over the harbour and among the inhabitants to a limited distance from thence into Freetown.

The liberated Africans, some of whom were landed sickly, and located at the new settlements a short distance to the westward of the town, as well as those who resided at Kissey and other villages up the river, and at the mountain settlements, with the European managers and missionaries, all enjoyed good health. The natives upon the Bullom shore, to the north-east of Sierra Leone, were also stated to be perfectly healthy.

The European deserters and discharged men from the Royal African corps, who were allowed to proceed home in merchant vessels, nearly all returned to the shore afflicted with this malady and died; whilst the troops in garrison at the new barracks on Tower Hill, including one hundred and twenty Europeans, remained quite well, with the exception of a few who had gone on board of some of the vessels, and were taken ill with the same fever, and died; as did Lieutenant Patterson of the African corps, and a commissariat officer, who had not long arrived from England.

This fever carried off persons who were attacked by it, in a much less time than the usual fever, which type the former gradually subsided into, as the rainy season advanced.

The First Ashanti Campaign
By J. W. Fortescue

The Rise of the Ashantis

The reader's attention must now be diverted for the first time to a new field of operations, of which, but for petty attacks and captures in the long struggle for empire against France, he has so far heard nothing. The British settlements on the West Coast of Africa had been originally established for the promotion of the slave trade; and the Royal African Company, together with its successor the African Company of Merchants, had ever since the seventeenth century sucked thereout no small advantage. The so-called settlements were simply fortified depots, and the jurisdiction of the governor or factor or chief (whatever his title) of each settlement extended no further than to the limits of his depot. There were tiny garrisons composed, since the end of the eighteenth century, of detachments of West India regiments and of the Royal African Corps, which latter was made up partly of coloured soldiers, partly of Europeans who had been relegated to its ranks lest a worse punishment—if a worse punishment existed—should befall them.

Nevertheless, there was no question of territorial dominance over any continuous strip of the coast. Other nations, French, Dutch and Danes, had likewise their forts intermingled with those of the British; and it should seem that in all alike the officials had to seek for emolument in private trade rather than regular salary. Herein, therefore, was a frequent ground for petty quarrels, which were generally ended by the death of one party or of both; or if not, were healed by the bond of common vitality, which could not but be potent in so deadly a climate.

The first attempt at true colonisation on the West Coast was made by a company of philanthropic men who subscribed large sums for the foundation of a settlement of liberated slaves at Sierra Leone, with a capital called by the name of Freetown. Zachary Macaulay, father of the historian, who had been an overseer in a Jamaican plantation, was the first governor; and though, within twelve months of his arrival, Freetown was destroyed and sacked by a squadron of French *Sans-culottes* in September 1794, he set the ruined settlement upon its feet again by sheer industry and resolution, and did not resign his post until 1799. A few years later Freetown became the military and administrative headquarters of the West African settlements.

In 1807 the Slave Trade was abolished; the occupation of the African Company came to an end; and after some years of hesitation their forts were in 1821 transferred to the British Government. The principal of these, which lay from eight hundred to a thousand miles east of Sierra Leone, were, from west to east, Cape Coast Castle and Accra. Immediately at the back of the Dutch settlement of Elmina and of Cape Coast Castle lay the country of the Fantis, and behind them again that of the Ashantis; and it so happened that at the beginning of the nineteenth century there had arisen a precisely similar situation to that which we have seen in Nepal and Burma. The Ashantis, like the Gurkhas, had established themselves as a formidable military power which, having subdued their immediate neighbours, threatened to come into collision with the British.

The Ashanti Army had raided the Fantis and reached the coast for the first time in 1807. They had stormed a Dutch fort in 1808; they had made a second invasion in 1816, and a third in 1817, dragging off thousands of Fantis to slaughter at their capital, Kumasi, and 1820. blockading Cape Coast Castle. The trade with the Ashanti country being valuable, the British government had endeavoured to adjust all differences by negotiation. The authorities at Cape Coast had advanced money to the Fantis to buy off imminent danger, and in 1817 a Mr. Bowditch had actually concluded a treaty with the King of the Ashanti. But a savage host in the flush of conquest is not likely to be stopped by words. The king, having brought to subjection another rival tribe remote from the coast, sent emissaries among the Fantis to report the fact, and to demand from them a tribute which should help to adorn his triumphal entry into Kumasi.

The Fantis in general complied, but the people of Cape Coast Castle refused; and on the 5th of January 1820, an Ashanti mission arrived at Cape Coast to repeat the king's demand with threats. Almost simultaneously a British envoy, Mr. Dupuis, proceeded to Kumasi and there concluded a new treaty, wherein it was declared that the natives of Cape Coast Town were subjects of the Ashanti king and must accept the consequences of this fact. Meanwhile the Ashanti mission remained at Cape Coast, though the natives there attempted to answer their claims by again borrowing the money required of them from the British. The situation became difficult and dangerous. Some would have it that the governor of Cape Coast had violated the treaty, though he himself threw the responsibility for the breach upon the Ashantis. To hold the balance between them is impossible, and any attempt to do so unprofitable. It must suffice that the government of Cape Coast Castle and the King of Ashanti were sharply at variance.

Meanwhile, to the great discomfort of the settlement, the Ashanti king rigidly interdicted all trade with Cape Coast; and his emissaries, still refusing to depart for Kumasi with the tribute that they had extorted, put forth further demands of jurisdiction over the natives of that settlement. Finally, in April 1821, one of these natives was murdered at Mori, to east of Cape Coast Castle. Thereupon the troops of the fort were turned out and marched to Mori, where they dispersed a mixed force of Ashantis and of Fantis friendly to them, with a loss of some fifty killed; and the king was then given to understand that he should not be suffered to interfere in any matters within the cognisance of the British government at Cape Coast Castle. For the moment he seemed to accept the rebuff, but he still forbade any commerce with that particular place, and in January 1822 sent a message to the British governor which could only be construed as an insolent defiance.

At this juncture arrived Sir Charles Macarthy, with a commission to be governor-in-chief of all the settlements on the West Coast and to take them under the control of the Crown. He was sprung from an Irish family which had taken refuge in France; and he himself had sought service with the British Army after the Revolution. His career had led him first to the West Indian campaigns of 1795 and 1796, then to a captaincy in the 52nd when Moore was training the Light brigade at Shorncliffe, then in 1804 to a majority in the New Brunswick Fencibles—a fine corps of backwoodsmen—and lastly in 1811 to the lieutenant-colonelcy of the Royal African Corps. In 1812 he was appointed governor of Sierra Leone; and in 1820 he received the honour of knighthood. He was a zealous friend of the negroes, and seems to have been extremely popular among them. Probably no better man could have been found to reconcile the sulky agents of the extinct African Company to the rule of the Crown.

His visits to the various forts occupied the greater part of the months of March, April and May, 1822, when he returned to Sierra Leone well satisfied with all that he had seen. In November he was rudely shaken by the news that a sergeant of the Royal African Corps, a *mulatto*, belonging to the fort of Anamabo, a little to east of Cape Coast Castle, had been kidnapped by Ashantis and carried away into the interior. In February 1823, it was ascertained that the sergeant had been murdered; and Macarthy lost no time in proceeding first to Anamabo and thence to Cape Coast Castle. On the 21st of February intelligence arrived that the Ashantis who had murdered the sergeant were at Dunkwa, twenty miles to northward; and, without any notice to the regular troops, the local levies of Cape Coast were armed and hurried off to the scene of action at nightfall. Whether by accident or the treachery of their guides, they blundered into an ambuscade, and, though they had at their head a few of the Second West India Regiment and at least three regular officers, they were fain to retreat, having lost about fifty killed and wounded.

The result could not but be encouraging to the Ashantis; and the next message from the king, delivered to the Dutch governor of Elmina, was that the British would do well to enlarge Cape Coast Castle, as he intended to drive them into the sea. The next incident was the arrival of a party of Ashantis at Danish Accra to buy gunpowder, which party was intercepted by the British and dispersed with a loss of over fifty killed and some thirty prisoners. In June and July, Ashanti forces twice entered Fanti territory, but fell back upon the advance of British troops; and these last finally took up advanced positions at Nyankumasi, about twenty miles to north-east of Cape Coast Castle, and at Jukwa, about twelve miles to north-west of it, the latter station being occupied to prevent the Ashantis from penetrating to Elmina and obtaining from thence ammunition.

Throughout the closing months of 1823 Macarthy roamed from end to end of his government, heartening the waverers and encouraging the loyal among the native tribes, and finally returning to Cape Coast Castle at the end of November. His energy was indefatigable. He visited all the camps, walking most of the way on his own feet, presented colours to the Royal African Corps, and finally, upon the news that the Ashantis were marching in great force upon the coast, set out for Jukwa with the Royal African regiment, a small detachment of the Second West India regiment, and some native levies which passed under the name of the Cape Coast Militia. During the next few days he drilled his men in person, training them by sound of bugle to the work of forest-fighting, as became an old light infantryman and commander of backwoodsmen. Had he been as efficient in the business of transport and supply as in the theory of combat he might have gone far, for he was full of confidence in himself and knew not the meaning of doubt or of fear.

In the first week of January, 1824, his position was as follows. The enemy was understood to be advancing on a broad front in twelve parties. To meet them, one column, composed chiefly of native levies, under Captain Blencarne of the African Corps, lay at Accra, fifty miles to eastward. In Macarthy's own sphere of operations a part of his force, chiefly native levies under Captain Laing, was at Manso, having moved thither northward from Nyankumasi; and the main and principal body, of the composition already described, was at Jukwa. A large body of the enemy was reported to be advancing southward into what was called the Wassaw country, west of the Pra, which river runs into the sea about twenty-six miles west of Cape Coast Castle; and the King of Wassaw had massed his warriors near the east bank of the Pra at Ampon, about twenty-five miles to north-west of Jukwa.

Macarthy's orders were that Blencarne should advance northward from Accra, and Laing from Manso, to make diversions, while the main column from Jukwa should move to Ampon, whither he had already ordered one of his senior officers, Colonel Chisholm, to repair from Cape Coast Castle. He then designed to cross the Pra and strike in upon the left flank of the Ashantis' advance. For transport he depended upon native carriers, the only form of transport possible in a country where horses, mules, asses and oxen alike cannot live; and here he met with his first great difficulty. The natives asked an exorbitant price as carriers, alleging that their fellow-clansmen would despise them unless they shouldered a musket. Macarthy declined to pay these extravagant wages, with the natural result that at every favourable opportunity—and of these there were many during a march along narrow paths through tropical forest—the carriers threw down their loads and vanished.

The reserve of ammunition, under Mr. Brandon, the ordnance storekeeper, was sent round by sea to Sekondi, a little to the west of the mouth of the Pra, with orders to move up thence to Asamanka, some twenty-two miles to north-westward. Macarthy thought that he could venture to take this liberty, because his front to the west was covered by the friendly tribes of the Wassaws and Dinkeras; but it was hardly a sound arrangement to establish an advanced depot without a guard in a country which lay fully open to the enemy.

The bulk of the troops at Jukwa began their movement upon Ampon on the 4th of January 1824, marching in small bodies, owing to the difficulty of finding shelter and victuals. Macarthy himself was delayed by want of carriers until the 9th, when he set out on foot for Banso, a village seventeen miles to south-west, leaving eighty black recruits of the Royal African Corps, under an English ensign, one hundred and seventy black militia, officered by merchants of Cape Coast, and a rabble of two hundred natives under their own captain, to follow him. The troops and militia got into Banso the same evening, much fatigued; but the rabble did not arrive until late the next day; and the advance could not be continued until the 11th. By that time all the carriers who had come from Jukwa had disappeared; and the unfortunate brigade-major, Major Ricketts of the Royal African Corps, who was in command of the rear-guard, was obliged to impress carriers, male and female, and drive them along at the bayonet's point. There were a good many carriers and loads missing at the end of the day's march.

However, on the evening of the 11th the little column reached the Pra at Himan, and on the 12th descended the left bank over precipitous hills and across swamps more than knee-deep to the village of Daboase, eight miles distant as the crow flies. This place the troops reached late in the day, worn out with fatigue, while the rabble straggled along a considerable distance in rear. On the morning of the 13th, the troops crossed the Pra in eight canoes, each carrying one paddler and two passengers; and Macarthy caught up the company of Royal Africans, as soon as they had passed the water, and pressed on some fifteen miles to Akisuma, which, however, they and the militia reached not until the afternoon of the 15th.

Here Macarthy halted to allow the rabble to join him; and, learning that the Wassaws and another friendly tribe, the Dinkeras, were retreating before the Ashantis from want of victuals, he on the 17th summoned Jan. Chisholm to join him with his whole force from Ampon without delay. He also sent his colonial secretary, a Mr. Williams, westward to rally the Wassaws and Dinkeras and to mark out a camp for them. Williams found both tribes very unwilling to arrest their flight; and Macarthy was obliged on the 19th to send off, at a moment's notice, Ricketts with the company of regulars and the militia to stay them.

After a terrible march of twenty miles, under heavy rain and through mud waist-deep, Ricketts reached Williams early next day on the bank of the Adomanso. He arrived just in time to prevent, forcibly, with his militia the flight of the Wassaws westward across the river; and presently an alarm was given that the Ashantis were advancing. The Wassaws took up their position; messengers were despatched to warn Macarthy; but darkness came down without further sign of the enemy, and, as the Ashantis never fought at night, the weary host lay down to rest.

Early on the 21st Macarthy came up to the Adomanso, without his rabble, but with a bodyguard of two hundred Fantis which had been sent to him by one of the chiefs. He was absolutely incredulous as to the reported proximity of the Ashantis, and was in conference with the Wassaw chiefs when once again the alarm was given. The line was promptly formed, Macarthy's bodyguard taking care to remove itself as far as possible from him; and at 2 p.m. the Ashantis were heard to be within half a mile of the array. They were evidently in great force, for a native in Macarthy's army was able to certify the presence of many chiefs by the distinctive calls sounded on their horns. Macarthy ordered the band of the Royal African Corps to play " God Save the King," and immediately afterwards the Ashantis lined the opposite bank of the river, which was but twenty yards broad, and the action began.

The enemy attempted to cross the water by trees which had been felled to serve as bridges, but they were driven back with great slaughter, until at about 4 p.m. Macarthy's ammunition began to fail. He rushed to Brandon, who had arrived in the middle of the fight in advance of his stores, but could learn only that they had not come up; and in fact, despite the efforts of the escort, the carriers had thrown down their loads and disappeared. Furious with rage, Macarthy threatened to hang Brandon on the spot, and the unlucky storekeeper only saved his neck by incontinently concealing himself. The Wassaws by this time were in full flight; but the Dinkeras with the little party of regulars and militia were still fighting bravely, and Macarthy attempted to organise an orderly retreat. He was too late. The river had fallen until it was fordable, and the Ashantis, being four or five to one, were able to throw forward both wings and surround the few brave men who still held out. Macarthy, already wounded in two places, was speedily despatched, and with him eight other white men, either colonial or military officers, including Brandon.

Williams was disabled and taken prisoner. Ricketts, and the ensign of the African Corps, though severely hurt, contrived to reach the Pra with a certain number of the fugitives; and there, meeting an advanced party of European soldiers from Chisholm's force, they found themselves in safety. Of the handful of militia and regular troops with Macarthy, one hundred and seventy-seven were killed or missing and ninety were wounded, many of whom died later at Cape Coast Castle of hardship and privation.

Altogether the victory of the Ashantis was crushing; and they deserved it. They had completely outwitted and outmanoeuvred Macarthy, giving out that they were advancing in small divisions, whereas they were concentrated in one mass. Williams, while a prisoner in their hands, observed that their discipline and regularity in the performance of their duties was astonishing. There is no need to point out the faults committed by Macarthy. It is possible that some of them were forced by circumstances upon him; but perhaps his most striking lapse from military duty was that he sent but one single messenger on the 17th to summon Chisholm, and made no attempt to repeat his orders until the 21st.

Both letters reached Chisholm on the 22nd, within an hour of each other; when, realising the danger of the situation, he took a short cut by a bad path to the Pra. Since, however, he had but one small canoe in which to cross the river, the passage occupied the whole of the 23rd. On the 24th he made a forced march of twenty-one miles; and then, hearing of the disaster, he decided to retire to Cape Coast Castle lest the Ashantis should reach it before him. They had, of course, Macarthy's reserve of ammunition at Asamanka to replenish their stores, and would therefore be well equipped for such a venture. On the 25th, therefore, Chisholm re-crossed the Pra upon such frail rafts as could be improvised on the spot, thereby incurring the loss of yet more ammunition and a great quantity of arms, and reached Cape Coast Castle late in the evening. The British officer in command of the advanced guard died of fatigue before the march was well begun, which may give some idea of the ordeal undergone by Chisholm's force during these four arduous days.

On his arrival Chisholm found that Laing, having heard of Macarthy's disaster before him, had already brought back his troops to Cape Coast Castle; whereupon he decided that a force must be pushed out to meet the enemy farther from home. The native levies were, however, thoroughly scared; and it was with difficulty that some three hundred of them were induced to follow Laing, with a detachment of the African Corps, to Jukwa. Happily, the Ashantis seem to have been so much overjoyed through the capture of the depot at Asamanka that they lingered there for several weeks, and, so far as could be ascertained, meditated no advance until the 1st of March. There was therefore time to collect from Accra militia and native troops to the number of six to eight thousand muskets, and dispose them to defend the passage of the Pra, the right bank of which appears to have been occupied by the Ashantis from the vicinity of Asamanka to the sea. The British force, after passing in a few weeks from the command of Laing to that of Ricketts, now finally, owing to the sickness of these two officers, found itself under the orders of Blencarne.

Skirmishes—or rather, abortive waste of ammunition—occurred almost daily across the Pra; and the native levies, anxious to return to their homes, talked big of an attack upon the Ashanti camp, and began cutting paths through the forest in order to approach it. Blencarne endeavoured to dissuade them from so rash a venture, but, finding them inexorable, prepared to support them. The natives accordingly moved forward within striking distance, the enemy being quite unconscious of their presence, and seem to have been in a position to surprise the Ashantis completely.

At the last moment, however, they were seized with panic, swam back over the Pra, losing several men, two thousand muskets and a large quantity of ammunition in the course of the passage, and dispersed. The Ashantis, awakened by the clamour, advanced; and Blencarne, finding himself alone with his few regulars and militia, was fain to retreat on the 2nd of April to Cape Coast Castle. Such was the prevalence of sickness among the British officers on the Pra, that one only had strength to visit the outposts: and upon him accordingly the whole of this anxious duty was thrown.

On the 10th, by Chisholm's order, Blencarne moved out again to Afutu, eight miles north-west of Cape Coast Castle, pushing on such native levies as he could collect to Dompin, about the same distance to westward. There the Ashantis made a false attack upon them on the 25th of April, drew them forward by a feigned retreat of their centre and then, wheeling both flanks upon them, destroyed many and scattered the remnant in flight. Blencarne advanced at once to the sound of the firing, but arrived too late; and, hearing that the enemy was cutting paths in every direction towards Afutu, he decided to retreat forthwith. Before the last of his troops had left the village, the Ashantis entered it and very nearly cut off a British officer and a few European soldiers in one of the houses. These, however, escaped, and forming a rear-guard, which apparently had not until that moment been thought of, beat the enemy back with some loss.

The advanced parties of the Ashanti army then moved to within five miles of Cape Coast Castle, and there halted to await the arrival of the main body. Chisholm arrayed such troops as he had over against them; and with much difficulty a force of six thousand men, chiefly natives, was assembled. Designing to attack before the Ashanti reinforcements should come up, Chisholm began to cut paths towards the enemy's position; and on the 18th of May he was heartened by the arrival of the king's ship *Driver* with reinforcements from Sierra Leone. Marines were landed to garrison the castle so that every soldier might be released to take part in the coming fight.

The action began at 1 p.m. on the 21st of May, when the attackers emerged from the paths in many columns in single file, to find that the Ashantis had cleared the ground before their line so as to obtain a good field of fire, and had massed themselves in the forest beyond. They made repeated attempts to turn the British flanks, but were beaten off at all points with heavy loss, and after five hours' fighting retired. But three thousand Fantis, who had stood out resolutely for the post of honour before the battle, had fled away in panic at the first shot, carrying tidings of disaster with them. The victorious troops were obliged to fall back for some distance in order to obtain water; and under the influence of this double discouragement the whole of the native auxiliaries dispersed. It was, therefore, impossible to renew the attack next day, as had been intended; and Colonel Sutherland, who had arrived with the troops from Sierra Leone, now took over the command from Chisholm, and withdrew his whole force, except a small party of observation, within the castle.

On the 28th the main body of the Ashanti army reached Afutu. Their old king was dead, but his brother and successor sent a message to Cape Coast that he meant to drive the English out and throw every stone of the castle into the sea. It was not until the 21st of June, however, that he advanced, and not till the 23rd that he displayed his whole force within sight of Cape Coast Castle. There was wild alarm in the fort. Five thousand native women and children, refugees from the neighbouring villages, came in and amid frantic confusion squeezed themselves through the wicket with piteous cries. Seamen and marines were drawn from the king's ship *Victor* and from the merchant-vessels in the roads to man the guns; and every preparation was made to meet a general attack.

But on the 24th the enemy drew back to their old position four or five miles to north-westward, and thence threw out strong parties in every direction to lay waste the country and destroy the villages even as far as Anamabo. In that settlement also there were terrible scenes. Women and children came flying into the castle, and there were soon more mouths than could be fed. Famine, dysentery and smallpox made havoc among them; but still the castle yard was so densely crowded that a man could not cross it without treading upon human creatures. The filth and stench were appalling; and heavy rain swept the foul matter into the tanks of drinking water. The troops were little better off than the natives. The very officers had neither meat nor flour, and but little rice. The men of the little garrison died daily from exhaustion, want of food and contaminated water. Had not a ship come in from Sierra Leone with provisions, every soul must have perished.

Yet the garrison of Cape Coast Castle could do nothing to prevent the devastation by the Ashantis. It numbered, besides a few militia and a very small unorganised native force, but three hundred and sixty men, of whom one-third were in hospital. However, on the 4th of July the king's ship *Thetis* arrived from England with a draft of officers and men for the Royal African Corps; and therewith the enemy called in their detachments and on the 7th once more concentrated before Cape Coast Castle.

The king's tent was plainly visible, and even his movements could be observed through a telescope, while his officers flaunted themselves in the uniforms of British officers and men who had been slain. It was an anxious moment, for ball was scarce, and every scrap of pewter from the houses, and of lead from water-pipes, roofs and ships had been taken to make bullets and slugs. However, on the 6th five thousand natives had arrived from Accra and other points to leeward, who were armed as well as the circumstances permitted, and set to work to cut paths towards the enemy's position.

On the afternoon of the 11th a skirmish led to a general engagement with no advantage to the enemy, who made further demonstrations of attack on the 12th and 13th, and kept their watch-fires burning all through the night of the 13th. But in the morning of the 14th it was found that they had retreated. They also had suffered from famine, smallpox and dysentery until discipline had failed and many whole bodies had deserted. The demonstrations on the 12th and 13th had in fact been made by marching the same men round and round a hill, from the forest into the open, from the open into the forest, and from the forest once again into the open. The Ashantis needed no instruction in the stratagems of war.

Even now they retreated no farther than to a distance of six miles, in order to purchase fresh supplies and stores from the Dutch settlement of Elmina. Accordingly Colonel Grant of the Royal African Corps, who had arrived from England on the 18th with a few gunners and rocket-men, approached the Dutch governor with a request to land troops there. The governor professed to accept the offer with thankfulness, but at the last moment declared that his natives would not permit the British to land, and that he could not control them. The fact was that, since the blockade of Cape Coast Castle, all the Ashanti trade had gone to Elmina, and the Dutch had made much profit of it.

So with the connivance of the Dutch, the Ashantis kept a safe base on the coast for their operations at Cape Coast Castle; and the war dragged on. Officers and men continued to die. Chisholm, who had served on the coast since 1809, succumbed to the climate at last in October, when on the point of returning home; and his death, lamented by all classes and all nations, threw a deep gloom over Cape Coast Castle.

In March 1825, there at last arrived what seemed to be a formidable armament, no fewer than three transports, containing European soldiers of the Royal African Corps from England, and two hundred men of the Second West India regiment from Sierra Leone, the whole under command of Major-General Turner. This officer, who enjoyed a great reputation for being able to handle the most intractable men, issued a proclamation to the effect that the Dutch at Elmina had better be careful, and that he would never make peace with the Ashantis till they ceased to claim tribute or subjection from the surrounding natives. This done, he sent the men of the Second West India regiment to the West Indies, no doubt by order, landed a few of the African Corps at Cape Coast Castle and took the rest back to Sierra Leone, where, within twelve months, he died.

However, the threat to Elmina was evidently potent, for the Ashantis did not again threaten the coast for a year, and then not at Cape Coast but at Accra, where the Danish governor had from the outset seconded cordially the British in their contest with their formidable enemy. The force assembled to meet this invasion included a detachment of the Royal African Corps, with three British officers; four disciplined bodies of natives each about one hundred and twenty strong under four European merchants of Cape Coast Castle and Accra, and a fifth body under a native chief. These, with one or two small guns and a party of rocket-men, formed the centre, numbering in all three hundred and eighty muskets, with some five thousand native levies upon either flank; the whole being under the command of Lieutenant-colonel Purdon.

Advancing twenty-four miles north-east of Accra, Purdon met the Ashantis, about ten thousand strong, on an open plain, near the village of Dodowah; and a general action began at 9.30 a.m. on the 7th of August. The plan of the Ashantis seems to have been to isolate, if possible, the little body of white men in the centre and envelop them, according to their usual tactics, on both flanks. They were partly foiled by a vigorous and successful onslaught by the natives on the British right, but they succeeded, by means of taunts, in tempting a part of the centre to advance four hundred yards, when breaking through the natives on its left, they poured a galling fire on its left flank and compelled it to fall back. Purdon, however, who had kept a small body in reserve against any such mishap, now threw it into action. A few rockets, fired at the right moment, spread terror and confusion into the ranks of the Ashantis, and some rounds of grape, poured upon the victorious enemy on the left, checked their onslaught.

The native levies rallied, and the whole line, advancing, bore the enemy back beyond recall. The fight was savage on both sides, the combatant natives pressing furiously to close quarters with the knife, and inflicting frightful wounds alike on the able and the fallen. The allies of the British had many wrongs to avenge, and they avenged them after their kind with unspeakable mutilation. By 1 p.m. all was over. Five thousand of the Ashantis had fallen, or had been taken. Their camp with all their gold and baggage was plundered by those who had been most backward in the fight; and their captives were hurried away beyond British jurisdiction to be sold as slaves. The loss of the British and their native allies was reckoned at eight hundred killed and a thousand slightly wounded; one European officer alone being hurt.

Such a battle-field had never been witnessed by British troops before, nor is likely to be seen again, with its wild turmoil of savages, mad with bloodshed, cutting, stabbing, ripping, with the scorching sun overhead, and acres of dry grass, kindled by the rockets, burning under foot. Night fell at last; and the British lay on their arms, lest the King of Ashanti should yet again try his fortune on the morrow. All through the hours of darkness was heard the wailing of the Ashanti women over their dead; and when the light came the enemy was gone. The Ashantis had been decisively beaten at last.

In September they sent envoys to sue for peace. The British stipulated that they should pay four thousand ounces of gold as indemnity and send two persons of high rank as hostages to Cape Coast Castle. The negotiations were prolonged for months and years, but were terminated at last in April 1831, when the King of Ashanti sent his son and nephew as hostages, together with six hundred ounces of gold as security for good behaviour towards the Europeans on the Gold Coast; and so, in the language of the Old Testament, the land had rest forty years.

It may perhaps be objected that this campaign, carried on by a mere handful of British troops, and those of the worst description, together with a horde of African tribes, hardly deserves to find a place in the history of the British Army. Yet it was carried to a successful issue by a few British regimental officers; and it is the British regimental officer who has conquered the British Empire. The Royal African Corps beyond question did not include, as a body, the choicest of his kind, nor were the men—outcasts on account of crime from other regiments—ideal representatives of the British private soldier. Yet there was such an officer as Chisholm, who was loved and respected by all, and there were others, such as Ricketts, who, having lived long on the coast, must have been sober, clean-living, self-respecting men to have for so long eluded death.

When, after Macarthy's defeat, Ricketts, exhausted by wounds and fatigue, staggered up to the two men of his regiment by the Pra, and asked them if they knew him, they could not recognise the ghastly face until he told them his name. And then they took it in turns to carry him on their backs for some miles to a village; and when, even then, Ricketts could not rest until he had found Chisholm, they made a rude basket, impressed a black man as guide, and made shift to carry him on their heads, slashing away the branches that impeded their passage. And this was in the stifling gloom of the West African forest, where white men are better accustomed to be carried themselves than to carry others.

Yet even there the sense of duty made the wounded and prostrate officer persist in finding the superior to whom he must make a report which was vital to the safety of the force and of the settlement. And the men, as usual, cheerfully fell in with the desire of their officer.

They may have been, both of them, criminals; they may have been doubly-dyed incorrigible scoundrels, with backs scarred by the lash and consciences seared with a red-hot iron. But when the time of trial came they did their duty, and more than their duty, as British soldiers.

ALSO FROM LEONAUR
AVAILABLE IN SOFTCOVER OR HARDCOVER WITH DUST JACKET

THE ART OF WAR by Antoine Henri Jomini—Strategy & Tactics From the Age of Horse & Musket.

THE ART OF WAR by Sun Tzu and Pierre G. T. Beauregard—*The Art of War* by Sun Tzu and *Principles and Maxims of the Art of War* by Pierre G. T. Beauregard.

THE MILITARY RELIGIOUS ORDERS OF THE MIDDLE AGES by F. C. Woodhouse—The Knights Templar, Hospitaller and Others.

THE BENGAL NATIVE ARMY by F. G. Cardew—An Invaluable Reference Resource.

ARTILLERY THROUGH THE AGES—by Albert Manucy—A History of the DEvelopment and Use of Cannons, Mortars, Rockets & Projectiles from Earliest Times to the Nineteenth Century.

THE SWORD OF THE CROWN by Eric W. Sheppard—A History of the British Army to 1914.

THE 7TH (QUEEN'S OWN) HUSSARS: Volume 3—1818-1914 by C. R. B. Barrett—On Campaign During the Canadian Rebellion, the Indian Mutiny, the Sudan, Matabeleland, Mashonaland and the Boer War Volume 3: 1818-1914.

THE CAMPAIGN OF WATERLOO by Antoine Henri Jomini—A Political & Military History from the French perspective.

RIFLE & DRILL by S. Bertram Browne—The Enfield Rifle Musket, 1853 and the Drill of the British Soldier of the Mid-Victorian Period *A Companion to the New Rifle Musket* and *A Practical Guide to Squad and Setting-up Dtill*.

NAPOLEON'S MEN AND METHODS by Alexander L. Kielland—The Rise and Fall of the Emperor and His Men Who Fought by His Side.

THE WOMAN IN BATTLE by Loreta Janeta Velazquez—Soldier, Spy and Secret Service Agent for the Confederancy During the American Civil War.

THE BATTLE OF ORISKANY 1777 by Ellis H. Roberts—The Conflict for the Mowhawk Valley During the American War of Independenc.

PERSONAL RECOLLECTIONS OF JOAN OF ARC by Mark Twain.

CAESAR'S ARMY by Harry Pratt Judson—The Evolution, Composition, Tactics, Equipment & Battles of the Roman Army.

FREDERICK THE GREAT & THE SEVEN YEARS' WAR by F. W. Longman.

AVAILABLE ONLINE AT www.leonaur.com
AND FROM ALL GOOD BOOK STORES

www.ingramcontent.com/pod-product-compliance
Lightning Source LLC
Chambersburg PA
CBHW022007100426
42738CB00041B/731